ALSO BY LEONARD MICHAELS

The Collected Stories of Leonard Michaels

Time Out of Mind: The Diaries of Leonard Michaels, 1961–1995

A Girl with a Monkey

To Feel These Things

Sylvia

Shuffle

The Men's Club

I Would Have Saved Them If I Could

Going Places

EDITED BY LEONARD MICHAELS

West of the West: Imagining California
(with David Reid and Raquel Scherr)

The State of the Language (with Christopher Ricks)

the essays of
Leonard Michaels

the essays of Leonard Michaels

FARRAR, STRAUS AND GIROUX

NEW YORK

FARRAR, STRAUS AND GIROUX
18 West 18th Street, New York 10011

Copyright © 2009 by Katharine Ogden Michaels
All rights reserved
Distributed in Canada by Douglas & McIntyre Ltd.
Printed in the United States of America
First edition, 2009

Library of Congress Cataloging-in-Publication Data
Michaels, Leonard, 1933–
    [Essays. Selections]
    The essays of Leonard Michaels.
       p.   cm.
    ISBN: 978-0-374-14880-5 (alk. paper)
    I. Title.

PS3563.I273E87 2009
814'.54—dc22

                                    2009010437

Designed by Gretchen Achilles

www.fsgbooks.com

1   3   5   7   9   10   8   6   4   2

contents

II. AUTOBIOGRAPHICAL ESSAYS

editor's note

These essays were written over a period of at least thirty years, though nearly half of them, including "The Story of Judah and Tamar," "On Love," "On *Ravelstein*," "The Horns of Moses," "Beckmann's Faces," "Masks and Lies," "The Nothing That Isn't There: Edward Hopper," "A Sentimental Memoir," "Writing About Myself," and "My Yiddish," were written in the last eight years of Lenny's life. Some pieces were composed in response to a specific assignment or request from an editor, but then rewritten several times in ways that generally extended their boundaries. Other essays were written for no particular audience, as personal reactions to a book read, a sculpture seen, or a thought reframed— experiments in understanding and feeling as much as attempts to describe or explicate. Their subjects vary widely, encompassing literature, philosophy, and the visual and musical arts, but nearly all of them contain a powerful concern with sense experience itself—particularly with listening and hearing, looking and seeing. This accounts, I think, for what a close friend of mine called the "sensuous immediacy" of Lenny's living voice in these essays, caught in conversation with the people, artists, thinkers, and works that he loved the most: from Saint Augustine to Shakespeare; from Spinoza through Kafka to Max Beckmann; from Michelangelo to Miles Davis; from the Old Testament to Aunt Molly. These conversations—even in the nonautobiographical essays—are always personal, focused on precise moments of encounter. They are concerned with feeling but impatient of sentimentality. They aspire to a state in which sensuous and aesthetic experience, memory and meaning, remain undivided. But most of all, they are the essays of a storyteller, with the attendant humor of storytelling not wrung out of them.

The essays published here are the ones I thought best represented Lenny's very particular craft and habit of thought. As already suggested, they often existed in several versions, reflecting his tendency to regard writing as an open-ended process in which the same subject might be investigated through a variety of narrative forms. Hence, not all the versions selected here are the ones that originally appeared in print. Certain quotations and names recur between and within the essays; I have made no attempt to remove these repetitions, as I believe this chorus of voices was essential to the drama of thinking and rethinking that made the essay a vital form of storytelling for Lenny. The collection has been divided into critical essays and autobiographical essays, though many of the pieces straddle these distinctions, blurring the boundaries between criticism and memoir and even, in a few cases, between essay and fiction. Lenny had long wished to publish a book of essays, and more than anything, I hope he would have approved of this collection.

———

I WAS GREATLY HELPED IN THE TASK of assembling different versions of Lenny's nonfiction by his daughter, Louisa Alice Michaels, whose appreciation of her father's writing and efficient bibliographical skills helped immeasurably to establish the body of work from which the final selections were made. I also want to thank Philip Weinstein, who was the first, and among the last, readers of the manuscript, along with Lenny's brother, David Michaels; Brent Cohen (quoted previously); Susan Levenstein; Eli Gottlieb; and Lorin Stein—all, like Lenny, exceptional readers. Their comments—often informed by their personal connections with Lenny and his work—helped shape my thinking about the manuscript throughout. Finally, I wish to thank Wendy Lesser, who was often the first publisher of Lenny's essays, and whose friendship has been one of the great pleasures and consolations of the past thirty years of my life. Her appreciation and affection for Lenny have been as much of a help to me as they were to him.

KATHARINE OGDEN MICHAELS

Umbria, Italy

I.

critical essays

what's a story?

I

THRUSTING FROM THE HEAD of Picasso's goat are bicycle handlebars. They don't represent anything, but they are goat's horns, as night is a black bat, metaphorically.

> *Come into the garden . . .*
> *. . . the black bat night has flown.*

Metaphor, like the night, is an idea in flight; potentially, a story:

> *There was an old lady who lived in a shoe.*
> *She had so many children she didn't know what to do.*

Here, the metaphorical action is very complicated, especially in the syllables of the second line, bubbling toward the period—the way the old lady had children—reflecting her abundance and distress. The line ends in a rhyme—do/shoe—and thus closes, or contains

3

itself. With her children in a shoe, the old lady is also contained. In effect, the line and the shoe contain incontinence; but this is only an idea and it remains unarticulated, at best implicit.

"Can you fix an idea?" asks Valéry. "You can think only in terms of modifications." Characters, place, and an action "once upon a time" are modifications deployed in rhythm, rhythmic variation, and rhyme—techniques of sound that determine the psychophysical experience, or story, just as the placement, angle, spread, and thrust of the bicycle handlebars determine horns, a property of goat, its stolid, squat, macho bulk and balls behind, like syllables of a tremendous sentence.

> *Lo even thus is our speech delivered by sounds significant: for it will never be a perfect sentence, unless one word give way when it has sounded his part that another may succeed it.*

Saint Augustine means perfection is achieved through the continuous vanishing of things, as the handlebars vanish in the sense of goat, as the dancer in the dance, as the bat in the night in flight.

Here is a plain sentence from Flannery O'Connor's story "Revelation," which is metaphorical through and through:

> *Mrs. Turpin had on her good black patent leather pumps.*

Those pumps walk with the weight and stride of the moral being who inhabits them, as she inhabits herself, smugly, brutally, mechanically good insofar as good is practical. The pumps vanish into quiddity of Turpin, energetic heave and thump.

Taking a grander view than mine, Nabokov gets at the flow and sensuous implication of Gogol's story "The Overcoat."

The story goes this way: mumble, mumble, lyrical wave, mumble, fan-
tastic climax, mumble, mumble, and back into the chaos from which
they all derived. At this superhigh level of art, literature appeals to that
secret depth of the human soul where the shadows of other worlds pass
like the shadows of nameless and soundless ships.

No absolute elements, no plot, only an effect of passage, pattern, and some sort of change in felt-time. The temporal quality is
in all the above examples; it is even in Picasso's goat, different parts
vanishing into aspects of goat, perfection of bleating, chomping,
hairy, horny beast.

The transformation, in this seeing, is the essence of stories:

A slumber did my spirit seal;
  I had no human fears.
She seemed a thing that could not feel
  The touch of earthly years.

Life is remembered as a dream, her as a "thing," and himself not
feeling. Amid all this absence is an absence of transition to the second stanza. Suddenly:

No motion has she now, no force;
  She neither hears nor sees;
Rolled round in earth's diurnal course;
  With rocks, and stones, and trees.

The transformational drama is deliberately exemplified, in the
best writing lesson ever offered, by Hemingway in *Death in the*
Afternoon. He tells how he forces himself to remember having

seen the cowardly and inept bullfighter, Hernandorena, gored by a bull. After the event, late at night, slowly, slowly, Hemingway makes himself see it again, the bullfighter's leg laid open, exposing dirty underwear and the "clean, clean, unbearable cleanness" of his thighbone. Dirty underwear and clean bone constitute an amazing juxtaposition—let alone transformation of Hernandorena—which is redeemed (more than simply remembered) half-asleep, against the blinding moral sympathy entailed by human fears.

In this strenuous, self-conscious, grim demonstration of his art, Hemingway explicitly refuses to pity Hernandorena, and then he seizes his agony with luxurious exactitude. Though he does say "unbearable," he intends nothing kindly toward Hernandorena, only an aesthetic and self-pitying reference to himself as he suffers the obligations of his story, his truth, or the truth.

The problem of storytelling is how to make transitions into transformations, since the former belong to logic, sincerity, and boredom (that is, real time, the trudge of "and then") and the latter belong to art. Most impressive in the transformations above is that nothing changes. Hernandorena is more essentially himself with his leg opened. Wordsworth's woman is no less a thing dead than alive. The handlebars, as horns, are fantastically evident handlebars.

II

IN CHEKHOV'S GREAT STORY "The Lady with the Dog," a man and a woman who are soon to become lovers sit on a bench beside the sea without talking. In their silence the sea grows loud:

The monotonous roar of the sea came up to them, speaking of peace, or the eternal sleep waiting for us all. The sea had roared like this long before there was any Yalta or Oreanda, it was roaring now, and it would go on roaring, just as indifferently and hollowly, when we had passed away. And it may be that in this continuity, the utter indifference to life and death, lies the secret of life on our planet, and its neverceasing movement toward perfection.

But this man and woman care, through each other, about life, and they transform themselves into the creatures of an old and desperately sad story in which love is the vehicle of a brief salvation before the sound of the sea, the great disorder that is an order, resumes and caring ceases.

The man's feelings in the story, like those of Wordsworth and Hemingway in their stories, are unavailable in immediate experience. He lets the woman go, time passes, then it comes to him that he needs her, the old story.

The motive for metaphor, shrinking from
The weight of primary noon,
The A B C of being.
The vital, arrogant, fatal, dominant X.

He goes to the woman's hometown, checks into a hotel, and is greeted by the sight of

a dusty ink pot on the table surmounted by a headless rider, holding his hat in his raised hand . . .

A metaphor. To find his heart, he lost his head. Nothing would be written (ink pot) otherwise; nothing good, anyhow, and that is the same as nothing. "There is no such thing as a bad poem," says Coleridge. In other words, it doesn't exist.

The best story I know that contains all I've been trying to say is Kafka's:

A cage went in search of a bird.

Like the Mother Goose rhyme, it plays with a notion of containment, or containing the uncontainable, but here an artifice of form (cage rather than shoe) is in deadly pursuit of spirit (bird rather than children). A curious metaphysic is implied, where the desire to possess and the condition of being possessed are aspects of an ineluctable phenomenon. (Existence?) In any case, whatever the idea is, Kafka suggests in eight words a kind of nightmare—chilling, magnificently irrational, endless—the story-of-stories, the infinitely deep urge toward transformation. "One portion of being is the Prolific, the other, the Devouring," says Blake, a great storyteller obsessed with cages and birds.

III

THE ABILITY TO TELL A STORY, like the ability to carry a tune, is nearly universal and as mysteriously natural as language. Though I've met a few people who can't tell stories, it has always seemed to me they really can but refuse to care enough, or fear generosity, or self-revelation, or misinterpretation (an extremely serious matter these days), or intimacy. They tend to be formal, encaged by prevailing opinion, and a little deliberately dull. Personally, I can't carry a tune, which has sometimes been a reason for shame, as though it were a character flaw. Worse than tuneless or storyless people are those with a gift for storytelling who, like the Ancient Mariner (famous bird murderer), go on and on in the throes of an invincible narcissism, while listeners suffer brain death. The best storytellers hardly ever seem to know they're doing it, and they hardly ever imagine they could write a story. My aunt Molly, for example, was a terrific storyteller who sometimes broke into nutty couplets.

I see you're sitting at the table, Label.
I wish I was also able.
But so long as I'm on my feet,
I don't have to eat.

I went to visit her when she was dying and in bad pain, her stomach bloated by a tumor. She wanted even then to be herself, but looked embarrassed, slightly shy. "See?" she said. "That's life." No more stories, no more rhymes.

Published as "What's a Story?" as an introduction to *Ploughshares*, Spring 1986, edited by Leonard Michaels.

the story of judah and tamar

TAMAR IS AMONG THE MOST COMPLEX, practical, and effective
characters in the Bible. The story is about her relation to Judah and
his sons. First, she marries Er and then Onan, and both sons die.
Judah promises Shelah, the third son, to Tamar, but she doesn't
marry him. Instead, she seduces Judah. The consequence is strange
and Tamar begins to seem more like an agent of history than a
character.

We are told very little about her, rather as if the woman is
taboo and the reader is deliberately discouraged from wondering,
or becoming involved imaginatively with Tamar. Where does she
come from? Did she have sex with Er, her first husband, the oldest
son of Judah? What about Judah's next son, Onan? Does Tamar
have sex with him before he spills his seed on the ground? Were
both sons, who are slain by God for unspecified wickedness, homosexual? When Tamar goes away at the end of the story, where does
she go?

The story is brief, yet eventful. Major events occur in this order:

1. Judah gives his oldest son, Er, to Tamar to be her husband.
2. Er is wicked and is slain by God. We aren't told anything in particular about his wickedness.
3. Judah then gives Onan, his next oldest son, to Tamar.
4. Onan is wicked. He spills his seed on the ground, refusing to impregnate Tamar.
5. Judah promises to give Shelah, his third son, to Tamar, but she must wait.
6. Tamar doesn't wait for Shelah to become her husband. Instead, she puts on a veil and sits at the crossroads.
7. Judah comes along and thinks she is a prostitute. They agree to terms and have sex.
8. Judah learns that Tamar, his daughter-in-law twice over, is pregnant.
9. Judah intends to have Tamar killed.
10. Tamar proves to Judah that it is he who made her pregnant.
11. Judah reflects on the case and says Tamar is more "righteous" than he.
12. When Tamar is in labor it is determined that she is carrying twins. A hand emerges from her womb. The midwife ties a red cord about the wrist to make certain that the firstborn twin will be recognized.
13. But the other twin emerges first.
14. Judah does not want to know Tamar again, and she goes away.

The biblical story records events in a bleak, assertive style, without laboring over meanings. But events become meaningful as they become—at some amazing turn—stories, just as notes become meaningful, retrospectively, in a melody. The moral, like a melody, is open to interpretation.

Talking about stories, Samuel Beckett says, "The sun rose, having no alternative, on the nothing new." Beckett means there is only one thing after another, which is to say meaningless repetition, which is no story. There was a time, however, when the sun rose again and again on unpredictable amazements. A sense of this is contained in the formula "Once upon a time."

This crucial moment of mysterious transformation is at the heart of the story of Judah and Tamar. Soon after she is widowed for the second time, Tamar disguises herself with a veil and pretends to be a prostitute. The veil is the turning point in the story, and appropriate to Tamar, an agent of divine power who moves amid mysteries.

When Judah realizes that he's been tricked into having sex with his daughter-in-law, he might have been outraged, but he decides, according to ancient law, that Tamar has done nothing wrong. Indeed, she has done justice to herself and made certain that the line of Judah is perpetuated, albeit through him, not his sons. When he states that she is more "righteous" than he, Judah's remark is legalistic, but it carries moral overtones. Perhaps Judah understands that Tamar has had enough of his wicked sons, and that she shouldn't have been made to wait for Shelah, who may have been as worthless as the first two.

By wearing a veil, Tamar doesn't merely seduce Judah. She obliges him to understand that she has been treated like a prostitute. In effect, the veil, hiding Tamar's face, reveals Judah to himself.

The hand thrusting from Tamar's womb is an amazement, since it doesn't follow from any previous event. It thrusts out of the story like an inexplicable excrescence, or a talisman of the wonderful. What follows the amazing hand anticipates and gives meaning to what came before as well as to the end of the story.

Tamar gives birth to twins who are the re-creation or redemption of Judah's two sons—Er and Onan—who were slain by God. Metaphorically and actually, then, Tamar is the mother of Judah's sons, both living and dead. Since the twin with the red cord was not delivered first, it means first is last and last is first, and this describes the paradox of Judah's fateful relation to Tamar. Judah is first—as the father of the slain boys—and last—as the father of their miraculous surrogates, the twins.

Veiled Tamar waited at the crossroads, a place that represents blindness to fate. Judah doesn't recognize her, the woman in whom his past and future lie. The veil of Tamar, a sign of prostitution, is also an invitation to the mysterious realm of storytelling in which meaningless repetition is transformed into meaning. In the realm of story, events assume a pattern in the otherwise arbitrary existential flux, and the sun rises on an unpredictable and potentially amazing future where there is justice for Tamar and redemption for Judah's dead sons. Judah, who doesn't want to know Tamar again, abandons her to the reader's imagination, which is our desire to know her.

A version of this was first published as "The Story of Judah and Tamar," in *Genesis as It Is Written*, edited by David Rosenberg (HarperSanFrancisco, 1996). The present version is Leonard Michaels's reworking of the original essay.

the story of jonah

I

STORIES WERE ONCE MEANT to be told and retold aloud. As in
the Bible, they were revelations of events on heaven and earth and
were the common property of the race.

Like fairy tales, they contained only a few immutable details,
making them easy to remember from one telling to the next.
Rapunzel has golden hair, but we don't know the color of her eyes
or how tall she is; and if you called her Baboonzel and gave her
black hair, it would still be a great story. The Frog King is handsome. This says merely that he looks nothing like a frog, and you
are free to imagine his appearance however you like.

Today, stories are written to be read, and sometimes in a way
that few people understand, leaving out most of the race. Furthermore, not everyone can read, and those who can do so in isolation
and silence, which is exquisitely sensuous but also alienating, perhaps a little scary since it smacks of magic.

When a modern story, which is written to be read in silence, is
read aloud before an audience, the experience is sometimes boring

and embarrassing. Events sound contrived, and the motivations of characters sound arbitrary. This is never a problem with old-time stories. When God calls Jonah and says, Go to Nineveh and cry out against the wickedness of that great city, it doesn't occur to you that this event is unconvincing. Jonah, amazingly, does not go to Nineveh, and perhaps you wonder why not, but you accept the action even if it remains puzzling.

The story of Jonah is puzzling, but it is also fascinating and has been retold innumerable times by writers and painters. Modern stories are hardly ever retold except in movies. The most extraordinary retelling of Jonah appears in a magnificently written chapter of *Moby Dick*, where a minister uses the story as the basis of a sermon. He loads the story with highly particular visual detail to make it real for his congregation, much in the manner of the Protestant clergy in his day. But it also seems that Melville, through this imagined minister, wants to make the story of Jonah uniquely his, to possess it slowly and luxuriously, swallowing it into the belly of this book, as the great fish swallows Jonah. But the great fish swallows Jonah in one bite, and the effect is terrific, whereas the minister chews long, and the effect is that of magnificence born of desperation.

I want to retell the story of Jonah, more or less as it is written, with emphasis on its repetitions, and the way the story tries to say the thing it cannot say.

II

GOD CALLS JONAH AND SAYS, Go to Nineveh, and cry out against the wickedness of that great city. But Jonah does not go to

Nineveh. He goes down to Joppa. Then he goes to the docks, pays
the fare, and boards ship for Tarshish, a city in the west Mediterranean, not in the direction of Nineveh and far away.

The ship is soon caught in a "mighty tempest," and the sailors
are terrified. They heave the ship's cargo into the sea and pray to
their gods. Jonah behaves again in a contrary way. He goes down
into the hold and falls asleep.

The shipmaster discovers Jonah in the hold and says, "What
meanest thou, O sleeper?"

Jonah is thus obliged to wake up and to explain himself. He
must say who he is, what brought him to this ship, and what
brought the ship into extreme danger. Challenged by the shipmaster, Jonah must suffer consciousness, which is Jonah's sacred afflic-
tion, because he is a prophet and consciousness is his calling. In a
sense, a prophet is not allowed to sleep.

The sailors discover, by casting lots, that Jonah is responsible for
the "evil tempest." Jonah says he is indeed responsible. He says he is
a Hebrew, he fears the Lord, and has fled His presence. The sailors
ask why. Jonah doesn't answer. He might have said that he could no
longer bear the fate of a prophet, which is to be forever sleepless
and conscious of God's will. Presumably, Jonah wants only a normal
life. It is also possible that Jonah, being a Jew, was frightened or dis-
gusted by the prospect of going to a city of non-Jews and crying
out against them.

For whatever reason, Jonah flees the presence of God, but then
Jonah hears the voice of God raging in the tempest. Jonah collapses
into sleep, as if to seek oblivion and escape the prophetic burden of
consciousness while others, in their ignorance, are terrified by the
tempest and throw the cargo overboard to save the ship. What a

dreadful loss, Jonah must have thought, and it is his fault. Out of guilt, he will ask the sailors to throw him overboard, too.

Finding Jonah asleep, the shipmaster thinks it's shocking and unintelligible, but sleep is simply consistent with Jonah, a man in flight from consciousness and God.

"What shall we do unto thee," ask the sailors, "that the sea may be calm unto us?"

Jonah tells them to cast him into the sea. This strikes the sailors as a hideous idea, not different from murder, and they ask Jonah's God not to make them murderers. They try to row Jonah ashore. The sea defeats their efforts. In their desperation, they can bring themselves to throw Jonah into the sea.

Jonah "went down into Joppa," then "down into the ship," then "down into the sides of the ship." Now Jonah is thrown down into the chaos of sea and swallowed down by a great fish that has been prepared for this moment by God. Since Jonah would flee God's voice and go down into the hold and sleep, there is justice in his fate, which he himself requested. If you want to sleep, Jonah, sleep there in the belly of the fish.

In the belly of the fish, Jonah sings the blues, and his theme is again about going down: "I went down to the bottoms of the mountains." Ultimately, in his flight from God, Jonah goes down into the deepest solitude, into the primeval wilderness, or what lies within himself. Insofar as he would flee the presence of God, who is other than Jonah, or outside himself, Jonah must descend into himself, what lies within. There is no place else to go. This doesn't seem a too fanciful idea if we remember that everyone, from little babies to adults, tends to go to sleep when under great stress.

The terrified sailors, who have never known the presence of God, cast Jonah into the sea, and "The sea ceased from her raving."

Then the men feared the Lord exceedingly, and they offered a sacrifice unto the Lord, and made vows.

Jonah is, thus, not exactly murdered but sacrificed to the wrath of God, and the sailors are converted to the Hebrew faith, which marks their entry into the prophetic world of Jonah. In this world, people, ships, storms, and great fish are the instruments of sacred imagination, and everything is metaphorical. It is the world where this can be that, the world of the one God.

The great fish that swallows Jonah is the metaphorical grave of the man who fled the presence of God. As in a dream, Jonah goes down into the belly of the fish, or into primeval creaturely being, the mysterious, visceral roots of mind, the source of everything that lives and must die. Just as the fish carries Jonah within itself, Jonah carries the fish within himself, for, in his flight from God, he has gone down into the sea and the fishy sources of the self. When the poet says, "I must go down to the sea again," he stirs a strange and melancholy yearning, reminiscent of homesickness. Not for the old neighborhood and house, but a much older place.

The fish carries Jonah about for three days, then vomits him onto land, and Jonah is restored to consciousness and the responsibilities of a prophet. God again says, Go to Nineveh.

Jonah, awakened and transformed, goes to Nineveh, and he cries out against the great city, prophesying its doom in forty days. God did not tell Jonah to say the city would be destroyed in forty days. But Jonah, having transcended his death in the fish, vomits death onto Nineveh, as if the wicked city, unconverted to the Hebrew faith and oblivious to God, must die just as he, Jonah, in his flight from God, was made to die.

Jonah sounds excessive, as if he were still terrified. Thus, he terrifies the citizens of Nineveh. They repent. Then "God repented of the evil, that he had said that he would do unto them; and he did *it* not."

But it displeased Jonah exceedingly . . .

He had gone about the great city crying, "Yet forty days, and Nineveh shall be overthrown." It seems that he now feels bitterly humiliated, but the story says only that he is displeased. In his displeasure, Jonah tells God he didn't want to go to Nineveh, because he knew God is merciful, gracious, and loving, and would repent of the evil He intended.

Jonah sits in the burning sun, outside the walls of the city, and refuses to leave until it is destroyed. The man who fled God's presence and wouldn't go to Nineveh now refuses to leave. Then, in a fit of suicidal petulance, Jonah asks God to take his life, "for it is better for me to die than to live."

God doesn't say: "Oh, come off it. I didn't promise to destroy Nineveh." He says:

Doest thou well to be angry?

The question is solicitous. But how can Jonah care? He has been allowed neither to flee the presence of God, nor sleep, nor die, though he has asked twice for death.

God then makes a gourd grow to protect Jonah from the sun. Presumably, Jonah is enclosed in the womblike belly of the gourd, as he was enclosed by the hold of the ship and the belly of the fish. The plainness of his response is very moving:

So Jonah was exceeding glad of the gourd.

Then God makes a worm, "and it smote the gourd so that it withered." Jonah should remember his gratitude for the gourd, and he should see that he is not essentially different, in his dependence upon God, from the gourd, and that his request for death is too despising of life. God reminds Jonah of his "pity" for the gourd, which is a reflection of Jonah's own pathos. God says you pitied the gourd

for which thou has not labored, neither madest it grow; which came up in a night, and perished in a night.

In other words, Jonah felt sorry for himself, and he should feel sorry for Nineveh. But he refuses to remember that he was "glad of the gourd," and he forgets his grave of three days in the fish.

And he said, I do well to be angry unto death.

Jonah fails to appreciate his own existence, which is at once everything and nothing, and the story ends as it begins, with God's voice looming against the silence of Jonah, for he has been thrown against the limits of his self, or his interior world, even as he was thrown into the sea and vomited onto the shore. God says:

And should I not spare Nineveh, that great city, wherein are more than sixscore thousand persons that cannot discern between their right hand and their left hand; and also much cattle?

If the ending is humorous, it is a humor of forgiveness, where God forgives His creature, or the superego forgives the ego for being what it is; and again Jonah must recognize the limits of his mortal condition, which includes limited understanding and death, the condition he shares with more than sixscore thousand persons of Nineveh and their cattle.

In his silence, perhaps Jonah feels the necessity of prophets in a world where people "cannot discern between their right hand and their left hand," and where people are not easily distinguished, in their ignorance, from the unconscious life of cattle. All life transpires in a kind of sleep, or darkness, or mystery. It is somehow critical to the existence of fish and gourds and beasts and people. It has been considered a form of grace, saving us from knowledge of what we are, and possibly how bad we are, or why anything exists or ceases to exist. The story of Jonah ends here, as if we have come up against mystery in the heart of creation.

WHEN THE SHIPMASTER SAYS, "What meanest thou, O sleeper?" Jonah answers that he is a Hebrew and has fled the presence of the Lord. But this is no answer. It is only a story, the very one we are reading. To answer, Jonah would have to say what it means to be a prophet, and why this fate seems to him so dreadful that he fled the Lord. But as a prophet, Jonah speaks for the Lord, not for himself. In his few words to the shipmaster, he offers hardly more than images of himself. But all the events in Jonah's story occur more as a series of images than as actions leading to, or entailing, one another. Things happen as they do in a dream, where images issue endlessly from the darkness within ourselves. When Jonah goes to sleep in the hold of the ship, perhaps he wants to sink into that darkness and let dreams come and deliver him to another story, another life. "Whereof we cannot speak," says the great philosopher Wittgenstein, "we must be silent." But it is also true that, whereof we cannot speak, we dream, or tell stories.

Published as "The Story of Jonah" in *Congregation: Contemporary Writers Read the Jewish Bible*, edited by David Rosenberg (Harcourt, 1988).

bad blood

EVER SINCE PLATO SAID poets must be evicted from the Republic and murdered if they return, things have not been good between poets and philosophers. By philosophers I mean theoretical persons, more or less systematic in language. Poets make language erotic. This is the main difference between them. The rest is scandal, a history of bad blood. Here are moments:

- Goethe refused to read Hegel, though Hegel wanted to be his friend.

- Rilke refused to talk to Freud.

- Blake hated Bacon, Locke, and Newton. "I must invent a system," he cries, "or be enslaved by another man's."

- In his elegy for Stella, Jonathan Swift claims she once shot a burglar and could refute the philosophy of Hobbes at any time.

- Wallace Stevens says, "Marx has ruined nature."

- To Nietzsche poets are disgraceful because they exploit their experience.

- Sartre's books on Genet and Flaubert, so analytical and fat, seem inspired by envious greed.

- Freud thinks Shakespeare is depraved, but says his plays were written by the Earl of Oxford.

Marx began as a poet, failed, and converted to philosophy—perhaps in self-loathing. Renowned for self-loathing are T. S. Eliot, who wrote a dissertation in philosophy, and Coleridge, who was ravished by the Schlegels. Keats belongs to this group, too; manifest poetical genius, he wondered if he was philosophical enough. Plato, who started this ancient violence, was himself a poet.

"Whereof we cannot speak, we must be silent," says the philosopher Wittgenstein in a mean little poem against poets. Negative thrust from "cannot" to "must" slams the sentence shut. Wittgenstein also says language is a scum on the surface of deep water. To put this differently, some things lie too deep for the scummy touch of words. In this at least poets and philosophers agree. Simone Weil says a poem is beautiful insofar as the poet fixes his mind on what cannot be said. Nietzsche says his ideas are less good after he writes them. Socrates never would write anything. Plato said a philosopher betrays himself by putting his ideas into words. Even Blake, a great loquacious poet, admits something not to talk about:

Never pain to tell thy love
Love that never told can be
For the gentle wind does move
Silently, invisibly.

Freud turned deepest silence into a medical industry based completely on talk, but he still saved a place for silence:

> *Even in the best interpreted dreams, there is often a place that must be left in the dark, because in the process of interpreting, one notices a tangle of dream-thoughts arising which resists unraveling . . . This is then the dream's navel, the place where it straddles the unknown.*

A silent navel appears in the voluminous Saint Augustine. Of all places, it appears in his *Confessions*. He remembers a conversation in which he and his mother achieved sublimity, relieved of words:

> *And while we spoke of the eternal Wisdom, longing for it, straining with all the strength of our hearts, for one fleeting instant we reached out and touched it. Then with a sigh . . . we returned to the sound of our own speech, in which each word has a beginning and an ending.*

They returned, sinking into miserable sound. In Wallace Stevens's poem "Waving Adieu, Adieu, Adieu," he redeems us from sound:

> *That would be waving and that would be crying,*
> *Crying and shouting and meaning farewell,*
> *Farewell in the eyes and farewell at the centre,*
> *Just to stand still without moving a hand.*

This poem is about living, or subsisting, in the prospect of death, without sound or action. The philosopher, says Plato, lives a dying life. "Imagination Dead Imagine," says Samuel Beckett.

When his mother died, Saint Augustine showed no sorrow to the mourners, but he couldn't hide it from himself or God, so he went to the baths and, in the obscurity of the vapors, let tears slide down his face. "What was it that caused me such deep sorrow?" he asks. Has there been a more desperate question? Teacher of rhetoric, Saint Augustine occupied "the chair of lies." He says this lying rhetoric is a mysterious gift, impossible really to teach, but since he pretended to teach it, he was a liar on two counts. You see why he yearned to be relieved of words. When his bastard son dies, Saint Augustine says nearly nothing. Hegel, Byron, Wordsworth, and Marx also say nothing or nearly nothing about their sad bastards who died young or otherwise disappeared. Is there a tradition of silence among philosophers and poets regarding bastards? Rousseau is an exception. He raves about his five or six bastards, as if there is no place in our lives whereof we cannot speak. But who believes Rousseau could have had bastards?

According to Hegel, to say anything is to risk annihilating your interiority. That is, to speak is to risk being understood or losing yourself to others. According to Valéry, there is no such risk, because a spoken word never says exactly what it means. According to Roland Barthes, the Marquis de Sade leaves nothing unsayable. Whereof we cannot speak, Sade speaks. Barthes puts it this way:

> To conceive the inconceivable, i.e., to leave nothing outside the words and to concede nothing ineffable to the world: such it seems is the keynote of the Sadian city.

When Wittgenstein says, "Whereof we cannot speak, we must be silent," he echoes the biblical injunction "Thou shall not take the name of the Lord in vain." The Marquis says, "Thou shall." About the human body, a character in *The Canterbury Tales* says, "Thy sound is foul at either end." This holds for the Marquis de Sade, who literally identifies one hole with the other. This whole question, entailing relations of speech and silence, appears in Beckett's story "First Love":

> *She began to undress. When at their wit's end they undress, no doubt the wisest course. She took off everything, with a slowness fit to enflame an elephant, except her stockings, calculated presumably to bring my concupiscence to the boil. It was then I noticed the squint.*

"Squint" means amblyopia, a crooked condition of the eyes. A famous use of it occurs in *King Lear*. He says, "Dost thou squiny at me?" Beckett's use of "squint" intends many things, among them a condition of the hero's eyes. They cannot, when the woman is naked, look at her silent place, a place he cannot even mention. She is naked, he mentions her "squint." Whereof we cannot speak, we make a joke. Beckett's hero gives "squint" above for one below. High is low, the image strong, the hero silent. Whereof he cannot speak bespeaks his silent place, which is at her "wit's end," not his. Now we know where one's wit's end might be. "Squint," being a pun, speaks twice while the hero is silent. Whereof we cannot speak, silence discovers a word. The Bible says this was true in the beginning. All real poets have said this, too, and all their work is a demonstration of its truth. It is no wonder that philosophers, insofar as they are committed to demonstrate the opposite, hate poets.

Beckett's hero meets the woman near the grave of his father. This is an obvious irony. Death, Silence, Love, and Holes begin to slither among words like blood among cells, quickening them. In a word Beckett squints at the world. Now hear Freud, voice of philosophy, applied to Beckett's subject:

It is worth noticing that the genitalia, the sight of which is always exciting, are nevertheless hardly ever judged to be beautiful.

Is this really worth remarking?

In one school of oriental painting, it is conventional to leave the centers of paintings empty. The central place gods may enter. Whereof we cannot/must not speak is then conceived by philosophers, poets, and painters as high, deep, and central. Could it also be in a corner? High, deep, and central means it is everywhere. Whereof we cannot speak is everywhere we are.

First published in *University Publishing*, UC Berkeley, Spring 1978; also nominated for a prize given by the Coordinated Council of Literary Magazines (a part of the NEA) in 1979.

on love

IN A SCARY LITTLE POEM ABOUT LOVE, William Blake begins
with a warning:

> Never seek to tell thy love
> Love that told can never be;
> For the gentle wind does move
> Silently, invisibly.

> I told my love, I told my love,
> I told her all my heart,
> Trembling, cold, in ghastly fears—
> Ah, she doth depart.

> Soon as she was gone from me
> A traveller came by
> Silently, invisibly—
> O, was no deny.

I confess immediately that I'm not sure what Blake means. The poem is chilling and sad. It seems to mean, if you're in love, best keep it to yourself; or, maybe it means you can talk about love, but the moment you do you aren't talking about love. Love is a mystery; otherwise it is nothing.

The poem suggests a good deal else, depending on what Blake means by love. Is it the kind that cannot speak its name? Whatever the poem means, it seems to intimate that there is something like an impulse, or a terrifying compulsion, to tell when one is in love, and that this impulse springs from a strange desire for the death of love, or maybe just death.

There are of course all kinds of love. Perhaps the kind that Blake's narrator talks about—and loses—might best be understood by thinking of its opposite, of exactly what love isn't: pornography, or the graphic demystification and annihilation of mystery. In other words, pornography represents the desire for some feeling to be exhaustively talked about or imagined or exhibited, which is probably the condition that the modern world knows best in regard to every subject: love, sex, food, etc. It's been said that we live now in a world of images and imitations, and that this is just as likely to be true of, say, the phony tomatoes in your salad as the passions in your heart.

Among contemporary novelists, the pornographic void has required incessant examination, and I don't mean only those novels that talk about sex. The novels of Henry James, for example, were considered obscene, or pornographic, by some critics of his own day because of their minutely detailed revelations of the interior life of his heroes and heroines. Tolstoy, a greater novelist, is a greater sinner. In *Anna Karenina*, he makes almost everyone who reads the book fall in love with Anna—thus preserving the mystery—despite the fact that she is narcissistic, self-indulgent, materialistic, irrespon-sible, inconsiderate, with bad taste in the men she marries or loves. Nevertheless, she is charming and gorgeous, and it is impossible for men not to fall in love with her, including Levin, who is surely Tol-stoy himself and knows better. Ultimately the mystery of love leads to her suicide, and the probable death of her lover, and the destruc-tion of her husband's career and moral character. In no other novel is the mystery so mysterious.

If we imagine a continuum from mystery to pornography, then it is possible to see where various writers might stand in relation to one or the other pole. Joyce, in his stories "Araby" and "The Dead," is close to love as mystery, while in *Ulysses* he is close to pornography. Nabokov's *Lolita*, whether or not you think it's a wonderful love story, is pornographic. This becomes paradoxically evident in the two movie versions of the novel, since neither ver-sion—however superb the directors or actors—features a heroine who is Lolita's age. If the beautiful girls were twelve years old, or even seemed that age, the effect would be sickening, rather like the flash of obscene white flesh that is Quilty's leg, offered to the cam-era by the always terrific Frank Langella in the later version. The flash is shocking, both hideous and funny. Adrian Lyne's intelli-gence and grasp of complexity in human feeling is rare in movies these days.

As it happened, during a course at Berkeley when I was enthu-siastically lecturing to students about *Lolita* the novel, a girl Lolita's age was kidnapped in a nearby town and raped and murdered. It became impossible then to carry on about Nabokov's fantastic wit, magnificent descriptive powers, and splendid achievement in the realm of lyrical imagination. A real girl was dead. The novel was suddenly nauseating.

You can sing, or you can write a poem, or you can find some other way of representing love-as-mystery, such as Manet's delicately sensational portrait of Berthe Morisot, or Freud's comment on what he felt when he saw Lou Andreas-Salomé's empty chair at his psychoanalytic seminars, or countless other examples that contain at least an instant of the unspoken and elusive thing.

Stendhal and Ortega y Gasset wrote interesting books on love, and later Roland Barthes wrote a book on love in which he says nobody talks about love. If it were possible to talk about love, it wouldn't be worth talking about: whereof we cannot speak, we take the *via negativa*.

"My mistress' eyes are nothing like the sun."

Love-as-mystery is in Shakespeare's "nothing." When another poet asks, "How do I love thee?" and then says, "Let me count the ways," it's a big mistake. Byron's "She walks in beauty like the night" is infinitely mysterious and much better, or Robert Herrick's "Whenas in silks my Julia goes" or John Donne's "Twice or thrice had I loved thee before I knew thy face or name." Love at first sight is an exciting idea, but, as Donne so beautifully indicates, love is prelogical or subrational. It is long before first sight.

In popular music, when the sublimely epicene Chet Baker sings "Let's Get Lost," or manly Nat King Cole sings "Your chick is all that matters," or the exhilarating Anita O'Day sings "You're the Top," or Miles Davis plays his agonized, drug-wretched, broken, and convincing version of "My Funny Valentine," they evoke moods of love, from deliriously happy to cool to witty to lead-heavy miserable. None is talking. They are artists being it.

The love moods, like Spinoza's modes of substance, are probably infinite. You can hear love's tragico-sublimity in Stan Getz's saxophonic big-balls sweetness when he enters amid Astrud Gilberto's singing of "The Girl from Ipanema." He virtually enters her. Sexual dependency is in Billie Holiday's "Fine and Mellow," a song she wrote. It was at the end of her career, long after the decline began, but only she could sing "Love is like a faucet / It turns off and on," and melt your heart. I happened to be present, with about fifty awestruck others, when she made the recording. She sang it twice. Dissatisfied with the first version, she said she wanted "more Lester" in the second, meaning Lester Young's solo saxophone. You didn't have to be a jazz aficionado to know this occasion was the thing itself. Not love as confession, but as a serious problem requiring high art for its expression.

In the movie *Farewell My Concubine* love is high and highly ritualized art, unrestricted by hetero- or homosexual determinations. As high art, the movie is reminiscent of Shakespeare's sonnets, where ritualized structure—fourteen lines, *abba*, etc.—becomes pure feeling. In the movie, there are scenes of magnificent Chinese opera where the dialogue is sublimed in piercing and unearthly cries. Very like love, the point of art is always not to talk, so that feeling might have its say. "When to the sessions of sweet silent thought," says Shakespeare in iambic pentameter. The problem of novelists, in this age of multitudinous blah blah, is how to keep their labors from devolving into talk, regardless of their subject, but especially when the subject is love.

There are all kinds of love, but I'm not talking about all kinds of love, only different manifestations of the kind in Chekhov's very great stories "The Lady with the Dog" and "The Kiss," or in Shakespeare's *Antony and Cleopatra*. Or even in these few quiet lines from Jean Rhys:

By far my nicest Cambridge memory was the day an undergraduate knocked me flat as I was crossing the road. I wasn't hurt but he picked me up so carefully and apologized so profusely that I thought about him for a long time.

What makes her last sentence wonderful is that it doesn't end at the period, but seems to abide in a sort of feminine and silent momentum. Don't you love her? For an analytical comment relevant to the hilarious and touching "nicest Cambridge memory," consider this from the brilliant, albeit heavy, Max Weber:

The erotic relation must remain attached, in a certain sophisticated measure, to brutality. The more sublimated it is, the more brutal . . . It is the most intimate coercion of the soul of the less brutal partner. This coercion exists because it is never noticed by the partners themselves. Pretending to be the most humane devotion, it is a sophisticated enjoyment of oneself in the other.

In short, never seek to tell thy love. Sartre, with his overheated vulgarity, schleps intimations of brutality toward love as sado-masochism. Not worth quoting, but without that sort of lugubrious theorizing talk, Stendhal makes the dark feelings scintillate in passages of lovely charm and wit in *The Red and the Black*, and, like Stendhal, but with inimitably evil subtlety, Henry James plays with brutal subterranean currents in *The Turn of the Screw* and *Portrait of a Lady*. No Chet Baker he.

I haven't read every book on the subject, but of late, when it comes to love at or around the mystery pole, it seems writers are in a pretty bad way, though Penelope Fitzgerald manages a brief and perfectly amazing flight in *The Blue Flower*, and John Bayley does somewhat the same in *Iris*. The former has the exquisite purity of idiocy. The latter is much more physical and brain laden, but, regardless of many differences, both end in unbearable pathos, which is not uncommonly associated with love's mystery.

In his book on silence, the excellent Max Picard sounds very like William Blake:

> *Lovers are the conspirators of silence. When a man speaks to his beloved, she listens more to the silence than to the spoken words of her lover. "Be silent," she seems to whisper. "Be silent that I may hear thee!"*

This is not to say "shut up," but only to say "stop talking." The difference is everything—in love and art.

Published as "On Love," in *Zoetrope*, Spring 2003.

i'm having trouble with my relationship

THE WORD "RELATIONSHIP" appears for the first time in the 1743 edition of *The Dunciad*. Pope uses it in a way both funny and cruel to identify his enemy Cibber with the insane. Cibber is said to be related to famous heads, sculpted by his father, representing despondent and raving madness. The heads were affixed to the front of Bedlam. Pope calls them Cibber's "brothers." Cibber and the heads have the same father; they stand in a blood, brains, "brazen" family "relationship." The word affects a contemptuous distance between Pope and Cibber and makes Cibber one with the sculpted heads. Funny in its concreteness, cruel in the play of implications, luminous in genius. Before Pope, "relationship" may have been part of daily talk, but until he uses it nothing exists in this way, bearing the lineaments of his mind, the cultural affluence of his self and time.

After 1743, "relationship" appears with increasing frequency, with no joke intended, and it not only survives objections to its redundant structure (two abstract suffixes), but, in the 1940s, it begins to intrude into areas of thought and feeling where it never belonged, gathering a huge constituency of uncritical users and displacing words that once seemed more appropriate, precise, and pleasing. Among them are "romance," "affair," "lover," "beau," "fellow," "girl," "boyfriend," "girlfriend," "steady date," etc. People now find these words more or less quaint or embarrassingly innocent. They use "relationship" to mean any of them when talking about the romantic-sexual connection between a man and a woman or a man, or a woman and a woman. In this liberal respect, Pope's use of the word is uncannily reborn.

People say "I'm having trouble with my relationship" as though the trouble were not with Penelope or Max but with an object, like a BMW, a sort of container or psychological condition into which they enter and relate. By displacing the old words for romantic love, "relationship" indicates a new caution where human experience is extremely intense and ephemeral, or a distrust of concrete words in which our happiness might suffer any idea of limit, or perhaps a distrust of words in general. It could be argued that "relationship" is better than the old words, since it makes abstraction palpable, generously distributing it among four syllables; a feeling of love in the actions of sex; or philosophy in desire. And, just as love is various, so are the syllables of "relationship," not one of them repeating another. Though intended to restrict reference to a single person, the word has the faint effect of suggesting any persons. In its palpableness, syllables bob like Bedlam heads. Strange images of mind.

People also say "I can relate to that" where no person is intended or essentially involved, just an idea of some kind of experience. The expression is innocuous, and yet it is reminiscent of psychopathic thinking. In the same modern spirit, people say "mothering" to mean no particular person is essential to the action; that is, "mothering" does not flow from a mother as poetry flows only from a poet, or life from the sun god. "Fathering" has a sexual charge different from "mothering" and cannot be used like this. We talk, then, of "parenting." The political necessity for "mothering" and "parenting," which justifies the words, doesn't make them less grotesque. But this sort of judgment is precious. The antinomies of our culture cling to each other like breeders in a slow, violent divorce, and aesthetic considerations are irrelevant. We have no use, in our thinking, for the determining power of essences, or depths of soul, or ideas of value that inhere, like juice in grapes, in the quiddity of people. Mom is not by any means an inevitable source of love. She might well be a twisted bitch, and many vile creeps are Dad. The words no longer pack honorific content. Commitments built into blood are honored only by the Mafia. Philip Larkin writes: "They fuck you up, your mum and dad."

What conservatives, feminists, Marxists, and other contemporary thinkers have in common is the idea that value has fled the human particular. Larkin might agree. He might even say that, long ago, value went off someplace to vomit and has not returned. If this is true, we have been abandoned to the allure of nonspecific possibility, or the thrill of infinite novelty. A lexical whorehouse shines in the darkness of the modern mind. (The "new," says Roland Barthes, is itself a value. No big surprise to the automobile industry.) To descend again to my theme: your hot lover has cooled into your "relationship," which in another aspect you have with your grocer or your cat.

This large disposition in our thinking and speaking arises from impersonal democratic passions, the last refuge of the supreme good. As Simone Weil says, thinking of God, "Only the impersonal is sacred." But it is a little crazy that "relationship," an uppity version of "relation," should be enormously privileged, lumbering across the landscape of English with prefix and two suffixes streaming from a tiny head of substance like ghostly remains of its Latin roots and Germanic ending (*referre*, maybe *latus*, and *ship*).

To have survived the guns of our grammarians and displaced more pleasant words in the natural history of English, it must answer an exceptionally strong need. The other words may seem impossibly quaint, but it isn't only the sophistication of "relationship" that is needed. It is the whole word, including the four-syllable sound, which is a body stumbling downstairs, the last two—"shunship"—the flap of a shoe's loose sole, or loose lips and gossip. In fact, "relationship" flourished in the talky, psychological climate of the modern century as we carried it from the offices of our shrinks and, like a forgotten umbrella, left "romance" behind.

Notice how the syllabic tumble of "relationship" makes a sound like sheer talk, or talking about something, emphasis on "about," not "something." Exactly here, in the eternally mysterious relation of sound and sense, "relationship" confers the dignity of thought upon referential promiscuity, its objects graced with interestingness, a sound basis in indeterminacy for interminable talk.

Philosophers might complain that it is a word without much "cash value." Heidegger, on the other hand, might take it as an expression of "the groundlessness and nullity of inauthentic everydayness." He means the nonstop impetuous trivialization, in "idle talk," of *Dasein*, by which he means anything real, by which he means that thing of which anyone who "is genuinely 'on the scent of [it]' will not speak." Certainly, then, in regard to "relationship," Heidegger might say:

> *Being-with-one-another in the "they" is by no means an indifferent side-by-sideness in which everything has been settled, but rather an intent, ambiguous watching of another, a secret and reciprocal listening-in. Under the mask of "for-one-another," an "against-one-another" is in play.*

By which he means, "I'm having trouble with my relationship."

"The secret king of thought," forerunner of deconstructionism, who spoke of the Nazis as "manufacturing corpses," Heidegger had the deepest grasp of what is authentic and inauthentic in human relations. (His literary descendants—as too often noted—manufacture "texts" out of "works.") But to feel what has been lost in thought, consider this text from a letter by Kafka to Milena, the woman he loved:

> *Today I saw a map of Vienna. For an instant it seemed incomprehensible to me that they had built such a big city when you need only one room.*

The incomprehensible city is "relationship," or what you have with everyone in the abstract and lonely vastness of our social reality. The room, all one needs, is romance, love, passionate intimacy, the unsophisticated irrational thing you have with someone; or what has long been considered a form of madness, if not the universal demonic of contemporary vision.

The city is also the "relationship" in the movie *Last Tango in Paris*, where Marlon Brando says to his lover, "Everything outside this room is bullshit." He makes the same point as Kafka, but the subtext of the movie is that, in our lust for relationship, we have shoveled all the bullshit into the room. This lust, which is basically for power, or control, or the illusion of possessing something that isn't there—*Dasein*, needless to say, but what the hell—makes us prefer Theory to novels, poems, and people, or flat surfaces in architecture to the various elaborations of material that once engaged our hearts.

Native speakers of Swedish say *forhallande* is close in meaning to "relationship," which suggests the Swedes are in the same boat as English speakers, especially since other native speakers say it is difficult to find a close equivalent to "relationship" in other European languages or in Asian languages. "Relationship," then, shouldn't be taken as a mere tendency of English where any noun might lust for sublimity in the abstract extension of itself. It isn't just another polysyllabic fascist on the left or right. Rather its use bespeaks a deeper tendency, in the soul, like what one sees in Andy Warhol's disquieting portraits of Marilyn Monroe and Mao, their faces repeating and vanishing into the static quality of their "look."

"Relationship" has a similarly reductive force, ultimately even an air of death worship. The "aura of death," says Bataille, "is what denote[s] passion." It also denotes its absence, one might suppose, but this old notion isn't likely to seize our imagination, which is why "relationship" has slipped unnoticed into astounding prominence and ubiquitous banality. The word is no less common than death, and it is no less pathetically private; and we use it much as though, after consigning ourselves to the grave, we had lingered to love the undertaker, having had no such exquisitely personal attention before, nothing so convincing that one is.

Published in *The Threepenny Review*, Fall 1989, and in *To Feel These Things* (Mercury House, 1993).

on *ravelstein*

Someone has died. What has happened? Nothing, perhaps, and perhaps everything . . . What can any human being mean to another?
—GEORG LUKÁCS, *Soul and Form*

SAUL BELLOW'S NOVEL *Ravelstein* is about a professor of political philosophy and his friendship with a writer named Chick. There is very little narrative development, but the novel holds you with incidents, observations, reflections, and Bellow's conversational style. His descriptive powers are also fully in play. For example, this image of wild parrots roosting in Chicago:

> . . . an entire tribe of green parrots, tropical animals surviving a midwestern winter . . . slim sacks hanging from trees and from the crossbars of the timber, power-line supports. Like over-stretched nylon stockings, those nesting tenements where eggs were hatched, drooped as much as thirty feet.

You might wonder if such parrots actually exist in Chicago, but even if you saw them you might wonder. The novel is like the parrots: remarkable, mysterious, paradoxical. It raises questions that are never answered, and there are transitions from one thing to another so quick as to be imperceptible. You are carried forward by the music, not the logic, of Bellow's voice. There are also inconsistencies in the two major characters that seem more like evidence of their humanity than complexities of representation. They live, so to speak, more than they are written.

The spontaneity of life is on every page. Early on, talking about the failure of Ravelstein's university to honor him as a world-famous professor deserves, Chick says: "I may return to this subject later. I probably won't." In fact, he never returns to the subject. The word "probably" indicates that Chick is talking, which isn't the same as writing. To read this novel, you must listen. In the immediacy and freedom of a voice, it lives.

Chick says he has been variously urged, encouraged, obliged, and "ordered" by Ravelstein to write his biographical memoir. Chick thinks about biographies he might use as a model, but it is apparent that he doesn't need models. His problem is that he lacks the will to begin writing until five years after Ravelstein dies, precisely when the novel ends. Thus, within the imaginary world of the novel, no biography is written. But Chick talks so much about Ravelstein that the novel itself is a biographical memoir, albeit an ironical example of the form, especially because Chick talks more about himself than his ostensible subject.

Since *Ravelstein* is called a novel, it shouldn't matter that the title character resembles Allan Bloom, the recently deceased friend of Saul Bellow, and Chick resembles Bellow. In a memorial essay on Bloom, Bellow includes a good deal that reappears in the novel. It's impossible not to think of Ravelstein and Chick as aliases for Bloom and Bellow, and not to wonder how much of what the novel says is merely true. When he talks about his writerly art,

Chick suggests that ambiguity is its very nature. Again like the parrots—which are essentially pictorial, whether they actually roost in Chicago or only in Bellow's descriptive paragraph—real people become characters in his novels as if they had merely shifted along the continuum between existence and literature. This idea is emphasized when Chick says death is when "the pictures would stop." Parrots, friends, wives—all that Chick calls "existence"—is essentially pictorial to his eye, or mind, or heart, or as it lives imaginatively in his words.

Early and late, Ravelstein's voice is heard in its particularity. He comes strikingly to life in physical and psychological detail, but we aren't told he is sick with AIDS until well into the novel. By sad and terrible degrees, Ravelstein is then seen dying. There is no other Ravelstein story. He is an extraordinary presence and then he dies. Afterward, in the only sustained narrative section, Chick talks about his own near death of fish poisoning.

In this incident and throughout, the novel is much concerned with the opacity of death, but the concern is unusually complicated. Chick says, "What I was to Ravelstein and Ravelstein to me. That was never entirely clear to either of us . . ." At the end of the novel, Chick suddenly produces a particularly vivid picture of Ravelstein, drawn from memory, years after his death. The picture culminates in this sentence, the last sentence of the novel: "You don't easily give up a creature like Ravelstein to death." Thus, in the picture, Ravelstein is still here. He lives in Bellow's pictorial art. There is perhaps a sense in which he never lived otherwise, just as there is a sense in which Chick never lives other than in the imagination of Ravelstein. Perhaps the question of what they were to each other goes unanswered except by the novel itself, in which, in their relationship, the two men live.

Though called *Ravelstein*, much of the book centers on Chick's two marriages, particularly the character of his beautiful, sexy, faithless, ambitious, competitive former wife. Strangely, he makes few comments about Ravelstein's longtime companionship with a young Chinese man named Nikki. As for Ravelstein's sex life, Chick calls it "irregular," but clarifies, "One had no reason to suspect him of irregularities of the commoner sort—the outlandish seductive flutters of old-fashioned gay men. I can think of no way to convey Ravelstein's normalcy. He couldn't bear the fluttering of effeminate men." The repetition expresses Chick's unwillingness to engage the matter and says more about Chick than Ravelstein. Later, briefly, Ravelstein's sexual adventurism comes up in conversation between the two friends:

Ravelstein says, "Chick, I need a check drawn. It's not a lot. Five hundred bucks."

"Why can't you write it yourself?"

"I want to avoid trouble with Nikki. He'd see the check stub."

Chick wonders if a visitor to Ravelstein's apartment stole something and then required Ravelstein to buy it back, but whatever happened would be less interesting than Ravelstein's remark about death being "a weird aphrodisiac." Not only for himself. That he is "dangerous," or infectious, is exciting to others.

Chick talks about Ravelstein's appearance, attitudes, ideas, beliefs, personal habits, prejudices, and rages, but the picture remains largely external, and contains little that might not have been known to other people. He calls it "natural history." But Chick also says he knows things about Ravelstein that must remain secret. Explicitly, then, Chick says he is unlike Ravelstein, who loved gossip and couldn't be trusted with a confidence. Presumably, Chick is making a distinction between gossip and a novel, or imaginative literature. Bellow is a great writer; nevertheless, if one cares about imaginative literature or friendship, the distinction might seem aesthetically and morally dubious.

As for Ravelstein's inner life, it is there mainly by implication or inference. Ravelstein himself was neither discreet nor reserved, and if you asked him to be direct, he "wouldn't spare you. His clarity was like a fast-freezing fluid." He believed "a man should be able to hear and to bear the worst that can be said about him." He preferred truth, even cruelty, to the sentimental distortions of kindness. Chick offers descriptive truth about Ravelstein, and some of it seems unkind, but he isn't cruel, and he betrays no confidences except when talking about his own personal life.

Amid many reflections on contemporary culture, the novel frequently notices anti-Semitism as it appears among the rich, the famous, the poor, and among Jews. According to Professor Davarr, who was Ravelstein's great teacher, the "vast collective will" to annihilate the Jews has made them witnesses to the absence of redemption in our world. (The name Davarr may be a play on *davvero*, the Italian for "really," or "indeed," or "truly.") An unredeemed world, recognized or not, implies nihilism. Ravelstein is admiring of people who can live their nihilism: "I like the kind who accept nihilism as a condition and live in that condition." He feels love for a Jewish woman who refuses on her deathbed to be visited by an Orthodox rabbi. "Nehamah was pure and she was immovable." Ravelstein then seems self-contradictory when he advises Chick to give serious attention to the religious heritage of Judaism, neglecting to say what he might discover.

There are places where Ravelstein makes unkind remarks about Jews. He even says the parrots have a "Jew look," but all the anti-Semitic material, silly or serious, including references to anti-

Semites in literature and politics—Céline, Voltaire, Lloyd George, Kipling, the Romanian Iron Guard—seems only a sort of mental background to the central complication of the novel, which concerns Chick's social relations with crypto-Nazis.

In describing his ex-wife, Chick says she was distant, cold, faithless, and had no sense of humor, didn't get jokes. Worse still, she obliged Chick, who is exceedingly conscious of anti-Semitism, to socialize with her friends, who had ambiguous relations with the Romanian Iron Guard. Ravelstein grimly remarks, "You're much too soft on people, Chick, and it's not entirely innocent either. There's an unspoken deal between you. Must I spell it out?"

Ravelstein doesn't spell it out. Chick prefers not to hear more. He repeatedly says, as if to justify his masochistic marriage, that Vela was beautiful. One might think of the movie *The Blue Angel*, in which an elderly intellectual falls in love with Marlene Dietrich, a vision of beautiful vacancy. Chick is masochistically obsessed with Vela's beauty. She is obsessed with it, too, checking her appearance in three different mirrors before leaving the house.

Nobody describes beautiful women better than Bellow. The best example is the debauched Angela in *Mr. Sammler's Planet*, who is apprehended in her moving flesh, her breasts, her odors, the sound of her brassy whisper, and her "fucked-out" eyes. She is the animalish counterpart of the black pickpocket who exposes himself to Sammler. Generally, beautiful women in literature exist more in feeling than seeing. They are not often pictorialized. Helen's face launched a thousand ships, but you never see it. The slave girl Breseis causes as much trouble as Helen, but you don't see her, either. Dante's Beatrice is made entirely of light. The eyes of Shakespeare's mistress are nothing like the sun. What does Dickens's Estella look like? Anna Karenina has black curly hair, a full figure, and small hands. How much does that tell you? As for Emma Bovary, there is reason to believe Flaubert himself wasn't perfectly sure what she looked like. You couldn't pick out any of these women in a police lineup, but Bellow's beautiful "bitches" would be easy to spot. Ravelstein doesn't think Vela is beautiful. His opinion is worth something.

In the novel *Herzog*, the beauty is called Madeleine. In *Ravelstein* she is Vela, another faithless wife. Madeleine sounds like madness. Vela sounds like veil, which is appropriate to Chick's marriage in regard to the way it serves to obscure things like Vela's Nazi friends or Chick's own moral character. Vela also sounds like *vei*, or pain, as in the Yiddish wail *Oi vei*. Herzog was humiliated by Madeleine. Chick is treated worse by Vela. After she divorces him he remarries and is enormously loved by his new wife, Rosamund, who is, like her name, a world of joy and hope.

Chick's own name suggests he is naïve, which is unconvincing but not intended to mislead. Chick is obviously sharp, complex, witty, and nothing if not Bellow. The name Chick is amusing and self-reproachful, but it describes an existential condition, a kind of "intimate metaphysics" or naïveté consistent with the belief that "the heart of things is shown in the surface of those things." Hence, the world is given to Chick in pictures or "epiphanies." Ravelstein thinks Chick's "distinctiveness of observation had gone much further than it should and was being cultivated for its own strange sake." Ravelstein "would probably" say, "Either you continue to see as a child . . . or you deal rationally with politics, with the city, with justice, with the fundamental problems." Chick says he would like to make himself fully known to Ravelstein "by describing my intimate metaphysics," but by then Ravelstein is dying and it's too late. Besides, Chick despairs of making himself known at all. "Only a small number of special souls have ever found a way in music or in paint or words to form such revelations."

As Chick talks, the novel wanders among his memories, sometimes repetitiously. Bellow is aware of the repetitions. It's the way people talk. If voice is texture, or the immediacy of life, it is being played against form, which has to do with artistic eternity. The parrots in Chicago—improbable, strange, irrelevant to events in the novel—are deliberately described twice, as if it were more important to note the mysteriousness of sensational existence than any formal presentation of a rational, consecutive order of events. Indeed, the novel observes no such order. It begins in the present moment with Ravelstein vibrantly alive, then shifts to the past. When Chick mentions that Ravelstein, increasingly sick with AIDS, has died, it is surprising and painful news. But, again like life, the novel merely continues and arrives at the only sustained narrative section. Chick tells of his near death of fish poisoning.

The story is taken from Bellow's actual experience, but it is made largely metaphorical. Here is Chick on vacation in the Caribbean: "The sand underfoot [was] ridged as the surface of the sea . . . and inside the mouth the hard palate had its ridges too." The transition from sand to mouth is weird and extremely brilliant. The mouth "inside" which Chick is standing alludes to Jonah, who was swallowed by the death-fish. Of course it is Chick who swallows the death-fish, but like Jonah he hallucinates in the belly of death, and is then saved. He is thereby relieved of guilt for having survived the death of his friend. At the same time, perhaps, in his metaphorical death Chick is punished and relieved of another guilt. It has to do with Ravelstein, of course; or with Chick's portrayal of him. The Book of Jonah, which is about guilt and redemption, is read on Yom Kippur.

Chick is exuberant in his praise of Ravelstein's intellectual achievements, his financial success, his great fame, and he reports the admiration of Ravelstein's students and important people here and abroad. Yet in other ways, the picture of his friend is so graphically truthful as to raise questions about Chick's feelings. His love of Ravelstein had a dark side. It would not be love otherwise. And it should be noticed again that the novel is wrought with contradiction. Chick, who can't write the biography, talks it. He and Ravelstein, highly self-conscious Jews, are impressed by nihilism in the Jew-hating novels of Céline. Chick, who cherishes understanding in friendship and love, is enthralled by a dull beauty associated with evil, and he evades Ravelstein's questions on this matter. A novel about Ravelstein turns out to be largely about Chick. But if this were a biographical memoir about Allan Bloom, instead of a novel about Ravelstein, the following picture would be inconceivable:

Ravelstein, says Chick, is a large bald man with long pale ugly legs, feet of unequal size, grossly shaped ears, and trembling fingers. As his name intimates, Ravelstein is ravenous. He devours knowledge, art, food, gossip, bodies. He is an insatiable Rabelaisian force incommensurate with an academic dedication. His long-term relationship with the young Chinese man has ceased being sexual, but in his relations with students, Ravelstein is more or less erotic, generous, mean, prying, fatherly, clinging. Chick says, as a teacher Ravelstein's mission is "to make certain . . . that the greatness of humankind does not evaporate in well-being," but in his passion for clothes, furniture, and food, Ravelstein appears addicted to well-being. His apartment is loaded with new, expensive, name-brand things. A huge espresso machine sits on his sink, making the sink unusable. There is so much expensive glassware that his cleaning lady can't do her job without terrors of breakage. Ravelstein, however, is more liable to break things than any cleaning lady. He is slovenly. He eats like an animal, spraying wine, "pawing" food onto the floor. He buys a four-thousand-dollar jacket and almost immediately soils it with coffee.

Ravelstein buys the best and costliest things, but his acquisitive passion is strangely hollow. For example, his exotic CD collection is played at top volume, as if from a boom box, advertising his refined taste to the whole building. Neighbors protest. Ravelstein thinks they are bourgeois types, wretched souls who deserve no consideration. But the bourgeois idea of possessions describes him better than his possessions. He collects paintings that have no personal significance except for being "right," and he hangs them in his apartment. Walls, he thinks, are made for paintings, and paintings for walls. One painting is of Judith decapitating Holofernes. She is a noble widow of great piety and propriety, probably not too unlike Ravelstein's bourgeois neighbors.

Ravelstein sends his expensive ties, which he has soiled in his slovenly eating, to Paris to be cleaned. Irrational extravagance amuses him, perhaps convinces him of transcendence, or higher materialism. But, as a deep critic of modern democratic culture, he seems like a super-consumer, a product of that culture, though he isn't democratic. He is dismissively cruel to students who don't measure up, and he thinks murderous violence in popular entertainment is a relief from our therapeutic concern to understand people. Blow them away. This idea, to his mind, is more comical than serious, but it is reminiscent of types who think as he does about therapeutic culture and would blow Ravelstein away. To some degree, the difference between Ravelstein and what he condemns is that he believes there is a difference. His higher materialism resembles higher narcissism.

He is a great student of Plato's *Symposium*, in which erotic longing, according to Aristophanes, is caused by our sense of incompleteness. Ravelstein's compulsive acquisitiveness of rare, expensive beautiful things suggests he feels incomplete. But Chick's repeated description of his wife as a beautiful thing fails to register sympathetically on Ravelstein, a collector of lovely objects. Since Ravelstein believes "a man should be able to hear and to bear the worst that can be said about him," it is imaginable that he would have relished a novel in which he emerges as a learned, intelligent, charismatic, somewhat megalomaniacal, comedic busybody as well as a loving, lovable, difficult friend who understands brutally, and doesn't understand.

In his contempt for what is no less true of himself than others, snobbishness and vulgarity coincide; but, unlike those others, Ravelstein has had the courage to put his authentic self into a book of ideas about the failure of modern democracy to meet the demands of the soul. Improbably, the book became world famous and made him very rich. Now, when Ravelstein goes to his beloved Paris, he stays at the same hotel as Michael Jackson. Bellow has long been a master of subtle comedy.

Chick encouraged Ravelstein to write his multimillion-dollar book. Ravelstein, in turn, wanted a biographical remembrance of himself written by Chick. Ravelstein's request is innocent but less than sensitive. It implies an equivalence between his best seller and a work by a literary genius. In the hospital, when Chick is forced to wear a restraining vest, he says, "It was killing me, binding me to death. I couldn't unravel it."

After Chick's metaphorical death, he is reborn, free of his former self. He feels unraveled, released from psycho-spiritual constriction by Ravelstein. Chick is prepared to write the biography. In the dazzling final picture previously mentioned, Ravelstein is seen dressing to go out for the evening. It is written in the present tense, and he comes amazingly to life, just as he does in his first appearance in the book, which is also in the present tense. Ravelstein puts on his expensive fashionable boots, and then his five-thousand-dollar suit. Pushing his boots through the pant legs of a five-thousand-dollar suit is what Ravelstein would do. The picture is endearingly grotesque and unforgettable.

When first seen in *Symposium*, Socrates is wearing new shoes. He doesn't usually wear shoes, but he has dressed to go out to dinner at the home of a handsome man. *Symposium* ends with Socrates rejecting the advances of Alcibiades. He chooses instead to talk, arguing that a man who can write comedy can also write tragedy. This applies to the final picture of Ravelstein, who couldn't seem more vibrantly alive in his comedic boots and suit, going out into the lethal night. Despite "the worst that can be said," it is immensely apparent that he is loved by his friend; and as long as Chick continues talking, he will not surrender Ravelstein to death. The novel has no formal ending. Chick is talking, in the present tense, when it stops.

Published as "On *Ravelstein*" in *The Threepenny Review*, Summer 2001.

legible death

IN THE SEVENTEENTH CENTURY, when the word "sentence" implied much more than it does today, Hobbes could write: "To hear a young man speak sentences is ridiculous." The word meant "moral truth," "wisdom," "pithy saying," even something like "numinous utterance." (*The Book of Sentences*, for example: a compilation of sayings of the Church Fathers.) "Sentence" also meant "legal decision" or "prevailing opinion of a population," as in "It is the common sentence of the people." The word could distinguish valuable substance from mechanical form—"What you say is full of good sentence"—but it might mean either substance or form: "The brainless boy read every sentence in the book."

In the nineteenth century, a philosopher makes these two meanings equivalent: "What a logician calls a proposition a grammarian calls a sentence." In effect, substance is surrendered to one sort of analyst, form to another. As for the old dignity, authority, wisdom, experience, learning, pith, numinousness—it no longer declares itself. "Sentence" has become silent as a corpse submitted to the analytical knife.[1]

A similar literary devolution, says Michel Foucault, occurred in the nineteenth-century medical clinic, where the individual patient was now being described in a language that rested upon "the stable, visible, legible basis of death." He was seen, in relation to his disease, as "only an external fact."[2] This new medical language was inconceivable earlier, because individuals were seen as mysterious incarnations of a vital principle, mediations of eternity, uniquely feeling beings, voices, persons. Foucault's idea of this linguistic innovation, inspired by Nietzsche, issues through the grin of a modern skull exhilarated by its own finitude. In any case, what happened to the way people saw one another also happened to the way they saw their sentences.

In our own time, Wittgenstein, a Father of the logical church, who is great for his compilations of agonized sentences, writes:

My only difficulty is an—enormous—difficulty of expression.

His reasons are implicit in many other sentences, but this one is dramatically revealing. "Enormous" swells in the middle and hangs by its dashes, and the word "difficulty" is repeated on the left and right of the dashes like arms. Between them the body, "enormous," pulls ponderously down. The problematic passion is within Wittgenstein, it seems, not history. He sounds lonely, crucified by his mind.

Though "sentence" is still used to mean decision—as in "The judge sentenced him to deadly labor at propositions"—its familiar modern application is to a unit of speech or writing. To be exceedingly precise, "sentence" now means "a series of words beginning with a capital letter and ending with a period, between which a subject and predicate are juggled, thereby signalling a thought." A young man speaking these will not be considered comical, only artificial. While we write sentences, nobody usually speaks them.

Indeed the modern idea of a sentence, though it includes many rhetorical possibilities, has no crucial connection with a voice, certainly not in the large sense of authority or origin. When President Nixon was told he had contradicted himself, his press secretary announced that the president's earlier remarks were "inoperative." There is really no such thing as a liar anymore. Modern sentences are generated in motions of the infinite gas, what some call "discourse," or the mumblings of depersonalized millions.[3] "I am not a Marxist," cried Marx too late.

A definition, then, of the voiceless modern sentence should emphasize its structural-visual character: "It is manufactured by alienated beings who know some words, the rudiments of punctuation, and are capable of what *looks like* a thought." "Sentence" must not also be considered an auditory phenomenon, something that necessarily must be heard—even through one's eyes—for the fullness of its occasion. Here, for example, Coleridge talks about listening, and thus hearing, through one's eyes:

> *The eyes quietly and steadfastly dwelling on an object not as if looking at it or as seeing anything in it, or as if exerting an act of sight upon it, but as if the whole attention were listening to what the heart was feeling and saying about it / As when A. is talking to B. of C.—and B. deeply interested listens intensely to A., the eye yet steadfastly fixed on C. as the subject of the communication—*

This is comparable to reading a sentence; the old kind; the old way.

Finally, then, "sentence" has not only fallen from its antique implications, it no longer has the slightest residual connection with *sentire*. "Sentence" is insensate. It bears no scent of presence, human or divine. A clean corpse. It is to be looked at, like modern glass-and-steel constructions, by nobody. It is wrought in the feelings, experience, learning of nobody. It is inspired by nobody. Furthermore, many modern nobodies insist that sentences are essentially meaningless, they have nothing to say.

To suppose any vanished implication or application of "sentence" might be revived, even if we all consented to try, would be nonsensical. Too much has changed. Even the poor word "sententious," which, to Samuel Johnson, meant "a lot of sentences," had already come to mean in his day an expression of scorn. Today, the mere sight of a lot of sentences may strike some people as an affront to sense, not to mention sensibility. Still, there remains an innocent, if melancholy, pleasure in reconsidering what we valued before we achieved modernity in legible death. To begin, please consider this sentence about the sentient body, by Martin Luther:

Faith resides under the left nipple.

We notice he does not say "heart" but substitutes a medical reality, "left nipple," for the pathetic banality, and thus, in a few particular words, makes his point terrific, his implication awesome.[4] A power—somewhat reminiscent of the power of God, residing neither in what we see nor literally hear—rings in these word things. The sentence does not signal to its readers, as if it were written for dogs. Nothing is signaled. Everything is, for Luther and for us, in the sense of this sentence. One might even say, in the desperate contemporary formula, "I hear you, Luther."

The comic drama of this next sentence, by Bertolt Brecht, also achieves great force of implication by playing with the relative proportions of a man and something hugely, ominously other:

The man who is laughing has not heard the news.

Compared to the looming, unspecified news, risibility is ridiculous, but, more impressive, the unidentified laughing man appears suddenly identified, naked as a nipple, so to speak.

Whereas Luther's sentence expands immensely by concentrating its focus, Brecht's sentence concentrates—showing us an idiot—by expanding its focus. They operate in verbal sound, or in the dynamics of voice, the way photoreceptive cells operate in the eye, seeking exact degrees of resolution through contrasts (background/foreground, dark/light, big/little, etc.).

These might be called sentences of visionary authority. If neither Luther nor Brecht says the very thing, what they say is nothing else. Therefore we "hear" it or "see" it. *It* is like a shadow, what Coleridge defines as subsisting in "shaped and definite non-entity." Derrida calls it a "trace." The difference is between absence and presence or everything and nothing. Tranströmer, the great Swedish poet, says, speaking of life these days, "often the shadow seems more real than the body."[5]

Less stunning than either Luther or Brecht, but more exquisite, is this sentence by Wallace Stevens which also does not say what it says so that we may hear it:

It is the word pejorative *that hurts.*

This isn't one of his famous or lovely observations, but it is supposed to seem less remarkable than it is. The sentence contains no hurtful word, only the category of such words, in *italics*, but—and this is its beauty—the sentence feels complete. It says all it has to say, even to our shriveled ears, without saying all. The feeling of completion comes mainly through the rhyme of "hurts" and "word." Auditory sensation carries a sense, the effect of closure, the effect of a hurtful word. Stevens avoids the possible vulgarity of a too particular word so that we may feel the pure impact of pejoration without the punch of a pejorative. ("It is the word *ratface* that hurts.") His sentence is the *sentio* of experience. Of course it is also a line, or what used to be called a "period," and therefore implicated in kinaesthetic feeling as well as sound.

Now please consider a famous sentence by La Rochefoucauld, which is also about pain, and, like Stevens's sentence, also faintly precious, reluctant to specify, to touch:

> *There is something in the misfortunes of our friends that does not entirely displease us.*

The vagueness of "something" is vaguely turned and refined by "not entirely," thus making the brutal sentiment nice, suitable—or sayable in society—and yet it is the kind of remark that might offend socialists.

Swift, who approved of La Rochefoucauld, nevertheless makes such vagueness vicious:

> *Last week I saw a woman flayed and you will hardly believe how much it altered her person for the worse.*

"Last week" is a journalistic *frisson*. It introduces lust for immediacy in looks and effects. The grotesque urgency of "how much" deepens the depravity in the voice of the sentence. You cannot read it simply with your eyes, the very instruments of abstraction responsible for "how much."

Again, this great sentence by Jane Austen requires you to hear its voice and the voice behind its voice, its genius:

> *It is a truth universally acknowledged that a single man in possession of a good fortune must be in want of a wife.*

She says a man in "possession" must be in "want," and her "universally" applies muscle to "single," tumbling it down the path to the anticlimactic "wife." The speaker seems, as if against her will, to suggest that being in want of a wife is the cause of good fortune. The same invincible willy-nilly marries that single man at the stop. The voice is officious, vigorous, funny, maybe a little depressed, and, in its push from exceeding generality through impotent individuality, gobbling up a world in words, finally thrilling.

For the sake of contrast with all of the above, here is a sentence by a young modern writer who would say the very thing, the thing itself, and not one word more:

> *I leaped to my knees.*

Near the exit of our sentence museum stand two sentences like sentinels. They are a splendid contemporaneous pair, from Hegel and Blake, saying opposite things, with equivalent cogency, in different ways. First Hegel:

> *The animal is the other in its agony.*

Blake answers:

> *How do you know but ev'ry bird that cuts the airy way,*
> *Is an immense world of delight, clos'd by your senses five?*

These sentences speak beyond the language in which they are written. "She sang," says Wallace Stevens, "beyond the genius of the sea." The internal rhyme makes the echo that is his meaning, and, while it might be imitated, the line cannot be easily explicated. Because the sentences from Hegel and Blake also have a form in which their intuitions are realized, and preserved against rational analysis, it is not easy to explain them without letting their energy and pleasure bleed away.

However, Hegel's idea of "the other" and "the animal" is given concrete elaboration by Ortega y Gasset. First he considers the monkey in the zoo—the way its nervous, fearful attention to the environment never ceases—and then he says:

> *Objects and events in its surroundings . . . govern the animal's life, . . .*
> *pull it and push it about like a marionette. It does not rule its own life,*
> *it does not live from within itself, but is always alert to what is going*
> *on outside it, to what is other than itself . . . [This] is equivalent to*
> *saying that the animal always lives in estrangement, is beside itself,*
> *that its life is essential alteración. ("Otheration.")*[6]

Hegel means consciousness without self-consciousness—"the animal"—is how we perceive "the other" in its distinction from ourselves, beings with an inner life, a self, capable of meditation, of ideas. The animal is imprisoned by sheer existence, or the forces of blind selfless existence. Agony.

Blake says self-consciousness is agony sufficient unto itself. The question form leaves Blake's sentence yearning, as if beyond the "five," though it is stopped hard at that word. Each sense, because it is countable and therefore definitively limited, is a prison bar. There is more to explain, but Kafka says our time is up. He concludes the Hegel-Blake exchange with a minuscule narrative sentence:

A cage went in search of a bird.

If we surrendered the substance of Kafka's sentence to a logician and the form to a grammarian, their analyses might discover the paranoic dynamism of our contemporary chemistry. It is, I think, the perfect modern sentence. Heavy with ancient resonance, and yet, in its radical form, immediate as this instant.

The sentence recalls Wallace Stevens's line about the motive for metaphor—"The vital, arrogant, fatal, dominant X"—being death. But Kafka's "bird" (freedom, life, art), like Blake's, seems to invoke its strange antithesis, rather than to be motivated by it. Neither of them is so concerned as Stevens to crush sentimentality; and Kafka's "bird," because it has less respect for logic, flies farther than Blake's. Literally preposterous, Kafka's whole sentence mimics the action of life, as if there were no other way to seize a certain weird, ultimately inexplicable, intuition: The meaning of life is that it stops.

NOTES

1. The first and second paragraphs are based, in a very general way, on definitions of "sentence" given in the *Oxford English Dictionary*. Only its quotations from Hobbes and the philosopher are reproduced. "The brainless boy" is invented. C. S. Lewis's *Studies in Words* (Cambridge, 1960), chapter 6, "Sense," treats "sentence" among several semantically related words, illuminating the historical

net of nuance in which they lie. Most of the exemplary sentences quoted later are translations. The original languages might not have greatly obscured the meaning of these sentences, but, in any event, what they gain in English is indispensable.

2. Michel Foucault, *The Birth of the Clinic* (Pantheon, 1973).

3. W. K. Wimsatt uses the phrase "infinite gas" in his book *The Verbal Icon*. The idea of iconicity is implicit in the discussion above, especially in the passage on Luther.

4. Stanley Cavell refers to this quotation in his very brilliant essay on *King Lear*, collected in *Must We Mean What We Say?* (Cambridge, 1969).

5. The quotation is from "After a Death," by Tomas Tranströmer, included in *Friends, You Drank Some Darkness: Three Swedish Poets*, trans. Robert Bly (Beacon Press, 1975). The stanza from which the quotation comes is:

> *It is still beautiful to feel the heart beat*
> *but often the shadow seems more real than the body.*
> *The samurai looks insignificant*
> *beside his armour of black dragon scales.*

The poem is much more complicated than my comment above suggests. It is about the effect of death in life or on life.

6. "The Self and the Other," trans. Willard R. Trask, in *The Dehumanization of Art* by José Ortega y Gasset (Princeton, 1968). Ortega does not say the following: The idea of Otherness is made into a noun that feels more concrete, "the Other." This noun is made to feel yet more concrete by identifying it with another noun, "the Animal." Passing back through degrees of concretion we return to the idea of Otherness, which is anything that is not anything else, or, most particularly, anything not the self. "The Animal," then, is the most interesting concretion of the life of the not-self, the living not-selfness which is "the Other." To be all this and conscious, but not to know it is all this, not even to know it is conscious, is the agony of the animal. (But animals dream. Dogs twitch, whine, and snarl in their sleep, as if they were running and fighting in an inner wilderness. This means they have an inner life? They are subjects or selves, perhaps even capable of meditation, like us? No; the way animals dream is the way we make sentences these days.)

Published as "Legible Death" in *The State of the Language*, edited by Leonard Michaels and Christopher Ricks (University of California Press, 1980).

the horns of moses

MICHELANGELO'S HORNED MOSES sits in a niche in a shadowy church. You can see the statue well enough despite the shadows, but the light isn't ideal for taking photographs. Nevertheless, camera people show up all year round, pushing through the crowd to get closer to the statue, as if it were a celebrity, the real Moses, rather than chiseled stone. It would be easier and cheaper for them to step into the shop a few yards away where you can buy inexpensive, professional pictures of Moses, made in good light. But they must take their own pictures of the majestic prophet looming large in the shadowy niche. One imagines that it gives them a sense of personal connection to the statue, so they shove through the enraptured crowd, which stands gazing in every season, and they press to the rail, focus cameras, and shoot. Some say it is the most photographed statue in Italy.

Camera people also collect in the Sistine Chapel, where you are specifically requested not to take pictures. But you hear continuous clicking. Taking these pictures not only strives for a personal connection, it is a kind of high thievery, albeit only psychological, but it must be particularly thrilling where it's not allowed. A clerical figure wanders amid the dense babbling crowd in the chapel, asking politely that people be quiet and not take pictures. They wait, these culture paparazzi, till he passes, and then the clicking begins again. The cameras sound like locusts eating the frescoed walls and ceiling, ravenous, never satiated. When the tourists lower their cameras, you sometimes see their desirous eyes tortured by a blood suspicion that others have something they want, even if they don't know what it is. Barbarians who overran Rome had such eyes.

The camera people who go after Michelangelo may be seeking a brush with celebrity, or more simply, reassurance that they have had an experience; but in the case of the Moses, where photographs are allowed, there may be additional motivations for their rapacity. Other statues, even some by Michelangelo, don't draw as many excited cameras, and Donatello's subtle, exquisite works inspire no comparable desire to take pictures. You can sit all day before his superb Magdalena, who stands in the Museo del Duomo in Florence, and nobody will click at her (even if both Moses and the Magdalena are remarkable for what the sculptors do with hair).

To photograph a work of art is to make images of an image. It is a way of honoring and trivializing it at once. Perhaps the horned Moses is too dramatic, too interesting, or too much to see all at once with the naked eye, and taking photos relieves you of the need to see things, let alone remember them. You see the heavy arms of Moses and the large hands, one touching his belly, the other his hair. You see the man's posture, erect and tense, and how his body faces you squarely while the head is turned to its left, the eyes cut left, glaring, angry. You see the curve of the mouth, how it suggests disgust and disapproval. And perhaps you wonder, since

Moses sees something terrible, why he doesn't confront it fully and directly. Does the glance to the left mean it is a distraction from more serious matters? What exactly does he see?

Moses remains self-possessed though taken aback, watching. Meanwhile, hair flows sensuously from his head all the way down his front. It makes the statue seem to exist in time, in the imperfect tense. I mean, the effect is temporal because, while Moses looks at the terrible thing to his left, hair flows through the fingers of his right hand. In effect, he was just sitting there when suddenly . . .

The body is powerful and male; the abundance and luxuriousness of his hair is female. It is mainly the hair of his beard, but it is not realistic. Being so lusciously fluent, it speaks for his passionate inner life. He seems almost to fondle his hair, which is a kind of action that has no intended goal, no necessary end. In essence, it is a gesture that remains essentially vague, incomplete. This is consistent with the story the statue illustrates. Moses is appalled by the behavior of the Israelites and will not complete the delivery of the commandments this time.

Though there are other portrayals of Moses with horns, Michelangelo's use of them is startling. The left one tilts oddly and looks damaged, and is, perhaps, a bit smaller than the right horn. They aren't new horns but old and damaged, animalistic, appropriate to a pagan satyr or a devil. Strange in the man who is carrying the tablets of the law dictated by God.

Michelangelo takes the horns from Jerome's mistranslation of a biblical passage. Where it says that rays of light issued from Moses' face, Jerome wrote horns, from which comes the belief that Jews have horns. Michelangelo was aware of the mistranslation but chose to put horns on Moses anyway, perhaps to suggest, in a sensational metaphor, how the Israelites betrayed Moses while he was on

Mount Sinai talking to God. Moses the prophet wears also the dis-
reputable, ragged ears of the cuckold. The betrayal occurs when the
Israelites collect their gold jewelry and make it into the image of a
bull calf, which they proceed to worship as if it were the god who
saved them from slavery in Egypt. The bull calf is an idol, or an
image, exactly the thing against which God's injunction stands:

> *"Thou shalt not make unto thee any graven image, or any likeness of
> any thing that is in heaven above or that is in the earth beneath, or
> that is in the water under the earth."*

The words are plain, neither gnomic nor metaphorical. They don't
invite interpretation. Michelangelo's horned Moses is about the
critical moment when the sin of image making, or idol worship, is
thrust upon the prophet's attention, and it has an obvious ironic
personal relevance to Michelangelo, an image maker. He is as dis-
obedient as the Israelites, and more so because of the more conscious sin.

As an image of Moses carrying the commandments, the statue
is not ambiguous. Each commandment is quite definite, telling us
how to live. Thou shall do this and not do that. They are resolu-
tions, not suggestions. They are final. But nothing in the statue is
final. It is alive with unresolved conflict. Mainly the conflict is
between unruly life and God's commandments. But even apart
from its religious significance, the statue is peculiar, sexually ambiguous in its hair, so free of proscriptions in its luxurious pour. A
man who has such female hair and unconsciously likes to feel its
flow, likes to fondle it, conflicts in feeling with the body's solidity
and its powerful arms and its expression of angry and uncompro-
mising disapproval.

The statue without horns would be less fascinating, less dramatic, less blatantly an image, and the conflict it represents less sharp or pointed, less like horns. The horns draw us in, scandalous in their dereliction, neither new nor newly acquired. In the cameras' clicking and whirring and incessant taking, it may seem that the biblical idea of betrayal is built into our condition, its giddy essence. If the animalish, pagan, demonic horns weren't there, camera people would feel less compelled to capture the mystery of the statue's indeterminate being. In some sense, however, the horned Moses can't be photographed. It can't even be seen, except from this or that angle. So you find yourself moving to the right and then to the left, or you try to get closer, or you step away from it for a different view. It cannot be held in mind, either, all at once.

A version of this essay was published as "Table Talk" in *The Threepenny Review*, Summer 1998.

beckmann's faces

There's no art
To find the mind's construction in the face.
—SHAKESPEARE, *Macbeth*

FROM EARLY TO LATE IN LIFE, Max Beckmann made self-portraits. They are a record of ideas about himself and his great art, much like a pictorial autobiography describing his passage from handsome inexperienced youth to the complex demeanor of his final years. He has been compared to Rembrandt, who also made a large number of self-portraits, and, again like Rembrandt, Beckmann sometimes painted himself wearing a costume. Both painters suggest there is something essentially theatrical in presenting your idea of yourself to the world. But Beckmann's self-portraits, unlike Rembrandt's, tend to have a kind of impersonality, or a severely objective air; and some might even seem detached to the point of self-alienation. In one self-portrait Beckmann leans aggressively toward the viewer, as if to emphasize fearless candor as opposed to intimacy or any deeply personal revelation.

Beckmann made portraits of others, too, and he painted and drew many faces that are not portraits but seem to be representative

social types of his metropolitan society. There are yet other Beckmann faces, more abstract allegorical beings taken from religious
literature or visionary experience, or faces that appeared to him in
dreams, some of them surely nightmares. Portraits or otherwise,
faces are an abiding subject of Beckmann's art. They appear in living rooms, cafés, and hotels. They loom in windows, looking into
rooms from the outside, or they are crammed into the corners of
large works. In one print, the surfaces of a row of cups bear faces.
The faces themselves show every sort of expression, or no expression, or one that is beyond interpretation. Some of Beckmann's
faces look at you as if they were suffering your attention. Other
of his faces seem oblivious to anyone's attention. Beckmann also
made strange figures without faces, or faces turned away from
the viewer: in effect, invisible faces. Whether sharply visible or
obscured, it is the remarkable indeterminacy of faces that fascinates
him.

This indeterminacy is merely true to life. A face looks different
from year to year, even from day to day. When it is incapable of
change, or slow to register change, a face can suggest a brain without a mind. Throughout Beckmann's work, dramatic values and
meanings are concentrated in faces, which are the essential data of a
social world. A face is the thing we most consciously bear or carry
into public view, while it remains invisible to ourselves; and it is
also the thing we contemplate endlessly in others, in the tremendous variety and subtlety of their moods, desires, and meanings.
The faces of others are what we love best, hate most, know best,
and least perfectly understand. A face is revealing and at the same
time a disguise. "A man may smile and smile and be a villain," says
Hamlet. A face may also tell us more than its owner knows, even
the opposite of what its owner intends. Whatever we say, our face

says it first, or differently, or withholds part of the meaning. It betrays as much as it expresses. It speaks of sadness when laughing, or satisfaction when commiserating. It speaks of feelings too subtle to be named, and yet they are instinctively, or unconsciously, understood by others. For no reason we can specify, a face can seem loveable or disagreeable.

The most indeterminate thing about your own face is what others see in it, which is to say qualities that are permanently invisible to you, just as what you see in others' faces is invisible to them. In photographs, we sometimes glimpse ourselves as seen by others. The face that is you then seems to belong much less to you than to them, and you begin to understand the extremely subtle way in which—like it or not—you are the creation of other people. This might have some bearing on why there is no society where masks have not been discovered.

Faces are like words. They are simultaneously personal and impersonal, multivalent, polysemous, opaque. We possess our faces but, as is also true of words, have only limited control over their expressive or revelatory nature. In a sense faces possess us, too, dragging us behind them toward the future, which they are almost always addressing. Faces, after all, look forward, continue speaking in the memory of others long after your words and their meanings are forgotten.

Where Beckmann shows a face in full or three-quarters, he sometimes puts another face beside it in profile, as if to say that people are inevitably isolated, or only partly seen in their relations with each other, or that it is necessary to keep something hidden. What isn't seen is both disturbing and, like lying, crucial to social life. In one portrait, Beckmann shows a face divided in half, one side lighted, the other in shadow. The division suggests that much about the woman is unknown not only to others but also to herself. Another portrait, entirely in profile, fills the page. It is monumental in effect, suggesting that the woman's public, visible, physical presence, as opposed to her mind, is all there is to say about her. She is likeable and depthless, not just superficial but also superfacial, like a movie star.

In Beckmann's sometimes crowded prints and paintings, or in his small groups, individuals hardly ever seem to look directly and fully at each another. Even if it is assumed the people he paints are bound by affection and love, what seems to connect them is not a mutuality of innerness but forms of sociality or formal self-presentation, the way people are connected when they collect in a living room or a restaurant.

Sometimes Beckmann's people jam together and yet have no apparent desire for community. His individuals just happen to be present in the same place. This sort of externalized connection is emphasized by the intensity of compositional factors, linear repetitions and tensions, or relations of light and dark. Thus, forms of conventional sociality and the impersonal compositional geometry of spaces and vectors become strangely equivalent. Pictorial space itself takes on a hard or vicious politeness, as if the interior life of individuals had burst into a frozen and severely binding community where everyone is isolated in his or her individual being seemingly coerced into a mechanical, affectless being-together and willful blindness to the existence of others. Beckmann also made pictures of people being murdered and raped in crowded rooms. In these pictures, one sees what connects people when forms of sociality break down.

Beckmann lived through the hell of both world wars, and many of his paintings and prints contain unspeakable horrors in which it seems merely to see was a challenge to his art. While most of his people don't appear to look at one another, there is one print that is very much about the experience of looking at a person. It is a nightmarish scene called "The Night" where three figures, two women and a man, study the sprawled, naked, murdered body of a man. He is on his back, half in bed, half on the floor, with arms and legs wide apart. His head is bleeding, part of his left arm is missing, and the stump is bleeding. The three living figures, presumably his murderers, seem to speculate wearily on the corpse. A hideous stillness prevails as they look at the man, but obviously they look only at a corpse, which is not exactly a person. Perhaps the lookers are not his murderers. Perhaps there is no implicit story and the picture says that merely looking at a person entails devastation.

Published as "Table Talk" in *The Threepenny Review*, Winter 1994, and later as "Beckmann's Faces" in the online magazine *ArtKrush*, edited by Wyatt Mason, 2003.

masks and lies

BOOKS ADDRESS THE EAR, a timeless organ. A movie imprisons your eyes. It acts on you, not you on it. Hence, you don't "see" or "look at" a movie. You *watch* it the way a cat watches a bird, until the cat strikes, kills, eats. Movie criticism often exhibits an aggressive, personal, killing response. In a famous attack on the movie critic Pauline Kael, much was made of her visceral responses to movies, as if these were inappropriate. In fact, they are most appropriate, since you watch a movie—a predatory watching—with the primordial intention of eating and killing. It figures that the basic form of movies, literally and figuratively, is the chase, and that people love to eat during movies, subconsciously anticipating the kill, the meal of blood. For the same reason, movie actors are more threatened by their audience than any other performers. No performer is more masochistic or suicidal. Marilyn Monroe, known for these qualities in her life and art, was "loved" to an extraordinary degree by the camera, the cannibal eye of her watchers, hordes gathered in the darkness, eating, eating. Too much was made of her sex appeal, too little of her oedipeal.

It's common for people not to read a book to the end, even when they like it, but very few walk out before a movie ends, whatever their opinion of it. I've known some who can't imagine walking out because they have never seen a movie they didn't like. They are pleased by the experience as such, which is easier than reading and essentially visual and passive. Quality is irrelevant. Nobody would say that about a book.

Unlike reading, it takes little determination to watch a whole movie, even one you don't like, since you need only sit still and not go to sleep. Besides, you often find yourself watching a movie with a friend who might like it, and then you can't suggest leaving. An argument over a movie can quickly become furious and threaten a friendship. Movies engage the most primitive sentiments. Books do, too, but people read alone and their experience is internal. Even when a person reads a book aloud to you, it's nothing like watching a movie with someone. Even going to a movie alone isn't like the privacy of reading. Movies are intended for the world—are fundamentally social and sensual—insisting on the physical senses of sight and sound. Words in a book make pictures and carry an author's voice, but these are miracles of interior sensation and belong to the radical privacy available only to human beings.

Some people dislike the privacy of reading, and wear earphones so they can listen to music at the same time. Some also dislike the privacy of others who are reading nearby. In an airplane, the person next to you may begin to make conversation the moment you open a book. I know someone who, when, as a child, she went to her room to read, was accused by her mother of masturbating. There is something about privacy—especially the silence and isolation of one's inner life as represented by reading—that can create anxiety or irritation in others. Today, in regard to ordinary privacy, the need to desecrate the thing inspires mass frenzy. The revelation of a little harmless fellatio between two chubby bon vivants affected the course of world history. I wondered about all this, particularly about the difference between movies and books, after watching Stanley Kubrick's last movie, *Eyes Wide Shut*.

The movie was received with much negative criticism, which seemed fair enough, but it had held my interest to the end, and later I remembered many of the scenes with extraordinary clarity. And yet, it wasn't so much the scenes that haunted me as the central metaphor, which had to do with masks. They appear in other Kubrick movies, too. Gangsters in *The Killing* wear masks, and so do the marauders in *A Clockwork Orange*. Apparently Kubrick was fascinated by them, but masks have been universally fascinating. They are important elements in plays, operas, novels, narrative poems, and many occasions of daily social life, as well as movies. Face painting and decorative scars are rudimentary masks in tribal societies. In technologically advanced countries, the cosmetics industry provides savage masks for innumerable women who won't settle for a natural face. Masks are so much in evidence everywhere that we hardly see them. Kubrick made them salient as objects to contemplate and as metaphors crucial to his thematic concern.

The origin of the word "mask" is itself obscure. The dictionary says it might be Arabic. If so, the word originates where the veil is worn, but there is no society in the world in which masks don't exist. They are often worn in religious and secular rituals—celebrations, initiations, festivals, balls, etc. The KKK notoriously wore masks and set fire to crosses. Judges and executioners have worn masks. The expression "death mask" refers to an impression taken from the face of a corpse. Thus, in death, a face becomes the mask of itself. We live and die with masks.

In one of the earliest stories in the Bible, a woman named Tamar disguises herself as a prostitute by putting on a veil and then seduces Judah, her father-in-law. In one of the earliest tragedies, Oedipus is deceived by fate into having sex with his mother. The stories are very different, but they have in common intra-familial sex when personal identity is obscured. Being literally or metaphorically masked makes possible what is, at worst, only imaginable. This happens several times in Kubrick's movie as characters seek sexual pleasure, with both comic and tragic effects.

In the ancient stories of Tamar and Oedipus, only Tamar is aware of the mystery she represents to others. Tamar's mask, then, is a deliberate lie. As such it is related to a pervasive social reality— that is, we lie to one another. In the most familiar and not very dramatic situations, as in ordinary conversation, in faint modulations of tone, you might discern fleeting minuscule lies, usually quite harmless, rather like minnows darting back and forth in a stream. Such lies make social life charming, polite, cheery, agreeable. Some have said they make social life possible. Dostoevsky wrote a funny essay on this subject, "Why Is Everybody Lying?" "What is a lie?" asks Byron. " 'Tis but the truth in masquerade." Another sense of social lying is in the joke about Hollywood agents: " 'Hello,' he lied."

We assume that politicians are liars, often vicious liars, but the entire social order is a construction usually based on some lie about national purpose. Fifty-eight thousand Americans, and millions of Vietnamese, were killed in war because of lies that our leaders told for no reason that anyone seems to remember. Perhaps this accounts for the media frenzy that would cast a blazing light on privacy, as if it were an evil darkness wherein lies may germinate.

Hermits are more painfully conscious of lies than the rest of us. They retreat from society and give their lives to prayer day and night, at least partly to escape the fact of continuous lying. In a hermitage there are strict rules of silence lest the hermits start, in the course of idle chatter, lying to one another. Christian saints urge us to attend with excruciating care to our most personal thoughts, for "the Devil is a roaring lion." This is an amazing image. It says we are susceptible to spiritual corruption, to the Devil's roar, in the intense silence and isolation of our minds. Hasidic rabbis were similarly obsessed, but assumed corruption was merely inevitable and urged us to persist, despite it, in the search for truth. "They are evil in their imagination," God says of the human race. Even if we weren't, it remains true that in the innermost sanctum, where we must go alone in search of truth, we are followed by bad society, albeit only one member, the Devil.

Despite its relation to lying, a mask isn't necessarily a lie, especially not when it is an obvious thing made of cloth, or carved and painted wood. A mask then obscures personal identity not to lie but only to create or preserve a sense of mystery, as in religious rituals that are sometimes accompanied by drumming, which effects a collective trance wherein the gods descend among people, and even enter their bodies. This obscuring of personal identity, this masking, is also fundamental to erotic experience.

In Shakespeare's comedies, lovers are often disguised, or metaphorically masked, and therefore happily deceived about personal identity, names as well as gender. Their ignorance, as in the stories of intra-familial sex, makes possible what is only imaginable. In traditional carnival—in such places as Venice, Rio de Janeiro, and New Orleans—a similar thing happens when the crowd becomes deliriously abandoned, free of personal identity, and then, with or without masks, amid universal estrangement, anybody might have sex with anybody. The old Italian word *carnelevare* derives etymo-

logically from "putting away or removal of flesh" (as in giving up
meat) yet contains the popular overtones of raising or "relieving"
the flesh on the eve of Lent. Similar to erotic estrangement through
masked celebrations, variations in facial features or skin color can
also become an alluring mask. Through a complicated transformation in genetic chemistry, the mystery of Otherness arouses sexual
desire. It has been scientifically explained as the desire for a sexual
partner outside of one's gene pool. That is, heterogeneity is crucial to
the health and survival of the species.

What effects estrangement, or obscures your identity in the
eyes of others, might obscure it from you, too, estranging you from
yourself. It is rather like what a child experiences when it covers its
eyes and feels invisible. People do things when feeling invisible, as
in a darkened bedroom, they couldn't do otherwise. In this way,
when masked, or mysterious to yourself, the imaginable becomes
actual, and sensual pleasure is suffused with the rapture of transcendence, as in miracles of art and religion.

Strangeness or estrangement, the essence of mask, is regularly
exploited for its dramatic value in all forms of storytelling, where it
is often a precondition of romance and sex. In Hitchcock and
countless other movies, in myth and fairy tale, in TV shows virtually anything that effects estrangement or liberation from personal
identity seems to carry some degree of erotic charge. *The Story of
O*, a highly sophisticated modern fairy tale, associates estranging
masks with the religio-erotic desire for humiliation. In *Blade Runner*
a man falls in love with a robot who will remain forever a romantic
stranger to him, and a mystery to herself, but the latter possibility
isn't explored by the movie. Basically, much the same happens in
The Stepford Wives, in which wives are murdered and replaced by

robots who the husbands find more desirable. In *Last Tango in Paris* strangers meet by chance and have sex instantly. In *Dressed to Kill* strangers have sex and, immediately thereafter, a homicidal moralistic transvestite appears who connects the masquerade of cross-dressing with sex and murder. Similar elements are at play in *Some Like It Hot*, but the transvestitism is hilarious rather than hideous and punitive.

Transvestite saints of early Christianity were women who cut off their hair and dressed like monks to escape marriage, transcend sexual identity, and dedicate themselves to spiritual love. The grossly erotic element reemerges when these women are unmasked and discovered to be women, sometimes beautiful. In ancient myth and fairy tales, personal identity is masked and thus transcended, as when a frog marries a princess, then turns into a handsome prince, or a sculptor falls in love with a statue and it then comes to life. Daphne, flying from sexual assault, reverses the sequence and turns into a tree. Zeus appears as a swan in the rape of Leda. The variations are innumerable, and so very different that any effort to reduce all the stories to an erotic algorithm will seem forced. But you have only to look at Bernini's impassive Apollo reaching for Daphne as she transforms, in horror, into a tree to feel the exquisite terror of estrangement at the core of sexual mystery.

Exotic travel affords another form of erotic experience, closely linked to the search for otherness. Thrills of estrangement are regularly provided in the TV classic *Star Trek*, which tells of travel to exotic places where Earthmen and otherworldly women sometimes become romantically involved and have sex. In the real world—though restricted to our small globe—many thousands travel to find love or to have sex with strangers. The strangers are sometimes children, which is pathetic and vile, but just this desire becomes high literary art in Thomas Mann's homoerotic romance novel *Death in Venice*. As it does also in Nabokov's *Lolita*, in which romance and lust converge in a story of exotic tourism and, unlike *Death in Venice*, actual sex with a child. The hero calls the child a nymphette and compares himself to an ape. Thus, he is among the swans, bulls, frogs, who are figures of lust, in myth and fairy tale. Otherness in the novel is represented by the child, Lolita, a figure of innocence, though it is suggested that she may have been around the block before the ape gets at her. Both the strangeness and eroticism of this story may have drawn Kubrick to make the first movie version of *Lolita*.

Imaginary as well as real historical tourists, like Odysseus, Byron, and Casanova, tend to be heterosexual, and they are drawn to women more often than boys, but Byron, like Casanova, had a lady lover who dressed as a man. In his narrative poems, Byron's heroes wear costumes, and when his great hero, Don Juan, hides among girls in a harem, he dresses as a girl. In Mozart's *Don Giovanni* there is disguise and sexual adventure culminating in travel to hell. Shakespeare's Cleopatra puts her "tires and mantles" on Antony, a sex tourist, while she dons his Philippan sword. Thus, cross-dressing and tourism, strangeness upon strangeness, or mask upon mask, figures in the most sublimely romantic tragedy ever written.

In life, mystery is desired and necessary, and masks have always been central to this. Yet modernity has been much about stripping off the mask—making the inchoate, the hidden, the invisible, visible. This modern disposition appears among the horses of Jonathan Swift's masterpiece, *Gulliver's Travels*, who are extreme precursors of

Nietzsche, Marx, and Freud—the great demystifiers who, largely, invented the world we now inhabit. The horses have no idea of mystery and believe that a lie is merely to say "the thing that is not." Living in a condition of absolute demystification, they are as unlike human beings as their counterparts, the Yahoos, are like them. Gulliver in the land of horses and Yahoos discovers that neither population—one supremely rational and the other depraved—is capable of wearing a mask. Gulliver then goes insane. This suggests that masks are necessary to the preservation of sanity as well as society in general.

It struck me, watching *Eyes Wide Shut*, that movies as a popular form have become comparable to Swift's horses. To put this very strongly, maybe too strongly, it is in the *nature* of contemporary movies—if not all individual movies—to demystify a great deal of human experience, especially sex, by making everything—especially sex—merely visible. There is hardly any aspect of existence into which the modern camera has not shoved its all-perceiving glassy snout. Like newspapers and television, movies teach us that anything is a potential form of entertainment, and voyeurism is an innocent depravity. Now we even know what Romeo and Juliet did with each other's body, what Anna Karenina did with Vronsky. Of course we always knew, and yet we didn't know, because the physical congress of lovers, before movies, existed in the haze of a reader's luxurious apprehension, or fantasy. There was always pornography, and nothing could be more intensely graphic or sensationally dramatic than, say, the prints of Hokusai, but still, something has changed. Before there were movies, for example, Bret Easton Ellis couldn't have written *Glamorama*, a novel in which sexual engagements are described in repet-

itive, graphic detail and motivation is a laughable idiocy. Compared
to Ellis, the Marquis de Sade's sexual cruelties, however lurid and
extreme, seem sentimental.

Thanks to movies, we know from the outside—from the camera's relentlessly neutral point of view—everything one body can
do to another for the sake of sexual pleasure, or that displeasure
which is also pleasure. It isn't simply that contemporary movies
mostly show us people being tortured, fucked, and killed; that
movies have convinced us that the technology of luminous revelation respects no mystery and makes everything in the world vulnerable to inspection. This conviction—true or not—may account in
part for the shock of all-demystifying hyper-journalism in the novels of Tom Wolfe as well as the ferocious contempt they have
elicited from literary critics, one of whom, at least, has put his fin-
ger on the problematic center. James Wood, in the *New Republic*,
compared Wolfe's last novel to Hollywood productions, particularly
in regard to the matter of illumination. Above all, this passion for
inspection is the enemy of metaphor; hence, much else that exists
only as metaphor. It reminds us that the visible has often been suspect, even sinful. They saw that they were naked . . . make no
images. Though Jesus repeatedly urged people to listen, hear,
understand, and believe, pictures and sculptures proliferated in
astounding abundance, as if none of the artists had much faith. Bot-
ticelli is an exception. After hearing Savonarola preach, he threw
his paintings into the bonfire of the vanities.

Stanley Kubrick's movie *Eyes Wide Shut* is an effort toward the
remystification of sex, obviously, and, by implication, a good deal
more. As indicated by the paradoxical title, the movie is about *not*
seeing. Men and women have orgiastic sex while wearing masks as
well as other disguises. The masks are large, sculpted things, remi-

niscent of Greek theater. They hide the entire face and remind us that masks have symbolized mystery from Sophocles to the Lone Ranger, or from a time when theater had the seriousness of religious ritual to our day of mainly frivolous entertainment. Kubrick uses cumbersome masks as a sexual metaphor that is radically antiromantic, since his masks make kissing impossible. But mystery beings don't often kiss. They ravish. This happens mechanically in the movie's orgy scene where everyone is masked, but only the women are seen naked up close. They appear naked in other scenes, too, as if to suggest mere nakedness has no erotic value. In the movie's hottest scene, the heroine confesses to an adulterous desire for a man wearing a navy uniform. A uniform leaves the face exposed, but it is only another kind of mask, hiding the man from the neck down. When the heroine has fantasy sex with the uniformed man, he never takes off his uniform, so the erotic charge of the fantasy is sustained. The thing desired is the mystery of desire, not penetration, certainly not the banality of consummation. She describes her desire, but the fantasy sex occurs only in the mind of her husband, who, in this respect, resembles Othello but without his murderous jealousy. In fact her husband seems only confused, and as if he had no strong feelings beyond curiosity.

The heroine desires the stranger because she is bored. She has a husband, a child, a grand Manhattan apartment, and she is beautiful. She has everything except mystery, the thing she wants. The movie ends with the husband and wife in a department store, which emphasizes the wife's boredom, or her sense of not-having amid so much that money can buy. She listens to her husband's plea for the salvation of their marriage, and she says a few words herself, and then abruptly says, "Let's fuck." She wants to make her husband shut up, presumably, because he isn't intelligent. Still, it seems a pity that the movie must end on this unfortunate line. But what is left to say? She has already confessed, in an earlier scene, that she would give up everything to be ravished by a stranger. Such longing has made, and continues to make, many go on pilgrimage, seeking ravishment by God.

The seeds of this essay appeared as "Table Talk" in *The Threepenny Review*, Fall 1999. This expanded version of the essay was never published.

the nothing that isn't there: edward hopper

Twice or thrice have I loved thee
Before I knew thy face or name

SHADOWY AND EROTIC, touched with savage reds, the painting
had the effect of a beautiful face. As with a beautiful face, I couldn't
get enough of it. I wanted to be alone with it, tantalized by a presence beyond what I looked at. I'd go up to the second floor of the
museum and look at Hopper's *New York Movie*. And look again. I
was sixteen and never owned anything valuable, but I could go to
the museum, be alone with the painting, almost possess it, or be
possessed as in a religious ecstasy by what isn't there. I thought *New
York Movie* is about desire for what isn't there, an effect of movies.

About that time in the forties, soon after Hopper finished the
painting, a movie named *Laura* was released, which was also haunting, literally about living with desire for what isn't there, the story

of a detective who falls in love with the portrait of a woman named Laura, a woman he has never met and believes is dead. The last thing we see is the painted portrait of the heroine, an image of the woman that the detective falls in love with before meeting the woman herself. It is this image, a phantasm forever inaccessible, which presides over the fate of all the characters, including the woman, and it makes no great difference if the murderer is finally revealed and the woman falls into the arms of the detective, since nobody can possess her image, the thing for which everyone yearns. But in the story, Laura suddenly appears. She isn't dead. The detective is shocked. I was also shocked, then tortured by jealousy. The detective might do something, even touch her. Played by Gene Tierney, Laura was a dream of endless desire. She seemed to me beyond possession. It was shocking to see that Laura was alive. It was also sad. Merely alive, then merely accessible.

Perhaps every movie is like *Laura*: that is, like a woman or the figure of desire in the house of desire. Hopper called his painting, which focuses on a woman, *New York Movie*, as if the woman were a movie, or the movie a woman. He had an erotic relation in mind, desiring what you see, desiring what isn't there.

Hopper was a painter of erotico-metaphysics as described by Plato. Hopper joked about being a philosopher, but he did read Plato. Like the ancient philosopher, Hopper was fascinated by what isn't available to our senses. In his mysterious paintings, he makes felt what isn't there, the nothing, the nothing that isn't there.

He was known to be solitary and thoughtful, like the blond woman in *New York Movie*. In the forties and fifties, it was easier to appreciate solitude than it is today. Hopper painted public places, rooms where people gathered, but usually with few people or nobody in the rooms. Few people in those days went to museums during the week, and the galleries might be vacant. You could stand before a painting for long minutes and not hear voices. There was silence in those days. It was associated with solitude, sacredness, internal life.

Silence and solitude were great themes in popular music, in songs like "Deep Purple" and "Old Man River," who "don't say nuth'n," or "Blue Moon" with the lyric "You saw me standing alone / without a love of my own," or the song "These Foolish Things," which carries a mood of solitude in almost every line. "A tinkling piano in the next apartment / Those stumbling words that told you what my heart meant / These foolish things remind me of you."

No stumbling now, no tinkling, no haunting presences. No indulgence in feelings that belong only to memory, feelings of not-having. Everything now is here. "In your face," we say, and "I want it now." We rap, we shriek in the raving crowd, and wear clothing big enough to hold two or three people, and walk about wearing earphones, or talking into cell phones, lest we feel alone. There are no philosophers. In Hopper's day we wore tight clothing and held each other close, saying nothing, dancing slowly, shuffling a few inches this way and that, feeling possessed, possessed by feeling. People preferred feeling to sex. You never saw graphic sex in movies. Now you see it all the time and there is hardly any feeling. People enjoy pornography, in which seeing and feeling are mutually exclusive.

I'd look at the woman in *New York Movie*, her blue uniform and elegant high-heeled shoes. It seemed her shoes were too elegant for her usherette uniform. They gave away her yearning for a life elsewhere. When the last show ends, she will take off her uniform, put on a party dress. She has a date, and they are going to a party.

Of course, she wasn't going anywhere. I mean only that there was drama in the painting, a kind of personal story, and it was more engaging, more psychologically intense, than the movie on the distant blurry screen, a rectangle near the upper left corner of the painting, like a window in a dark room. The usherette isn't looking at that movie, isn't involved with any movie drama, any mechanical story told with cuts and fades while music works on your feelings. Her drama is mythical, the myth of Eurydice doomed to wait at the edge of darkness. The red flashes in the shadows of the painting are streaks of fire and streams and gouts of blood. Eurydice stands at the edge of Hades waiting for Orpheus. This movie theater, like many others in Hopper's day, is called the Orpheum.

Hopper's Eurydice stands against a wall, holding her chin as she imagines the party she will go to later, in the Village, in a brownstone on Hudson Street, a short walk from the theater. She imagines the crowded rooms, high ceilings, and the air overheated by clanging iron radiators, reeking of beer and cigarettes. She sees herself standing in the kitchen, which is always the loudest and most crowded room, with a drink in one hand, a cigarette in the other, feeling slightly overdressed in those elegant shoes, which have begun to hurt her feet. But she is free of the usherette costume she must wear amid the Byzantine phantasmagoria of the movie theater, the place of the unreal where people go for a shot of desire and confuse it with life.

A man looks at Eurydice. She'd noticed him when she walked into the party. He'd been standing alone beside a tall window. The instant he looked at her she looked away and left for another room.

He'd followed, working slowly through the crowd, and now he was beside her in the kitchen. She ignores him. She is laughing because others in the kitchen are laughing. Someone had told a joke. She hadn't heard it, but she is laughing, making herself part of the ha-ha, unapproachable, but the man says, "Are you alone?" and there is terrible directness in his voice. She can't not turn, not look at him. "What?" she says, at once confused and pleased and frightened.

I felt such pleasing confusion, as if I were at a movie, when looking at *New York Movie*. But I would hardly ever look at a movie twice, let alone twenty times, as I might look at a great painting. Still, like a wonderful movie, Hopper's painting pulled me into itself, a drama that resisted understanding.

"A poem," says Wallace Stevens, "must resist the intelligence / Almost successfully." The same for a painting. Stevens's poems, like Hopper's paintings, suggest meanings, elusive as women who can't be had; at least not easily.

"Are you here alone?" he says. Eurydice says, "Go away, mister."

With his dark, gangsterish stare, the man resembles John Garfield but is taller, meaner-looking, and handsomer, though his skin is bad. Eurydice's mouth says, "Go away, mister." Her eyes say stay.

"Finish your cigarette," says the man. "We'll leave."

Eurydice says, "Pardon me?" and raises an eyebrow, at once quizzical and disdainful, and then she smiles coldly.

He waits with the patience of an intelligent animal, unsmiling. Eurydice lets her cigarette fall to the linoleum floor, which is sticky with spilled beer, and she tries to remember where she'd put her coat.

Women used to be virgins, so kids were shocked to learn what their fathers had done to their mothers. Now kids are shocked by nothing, bored by many things, and there is nothing they don't do.

In Hopper's painting *Two on the Aisle*, a man and woman are taking seats in a largely empty theater. The man is removing his coat. The woman is placing hers over the back of her seat. The moment is very ordinary, very plain. But then you wonder if the show is over. Is the man putting on his coat and is the woman reaching for hers? Are they leaving their seats, or have they just arrived? What Stevens calls "the plain sense of things" is anything but plain.

Stevens and Hopper looked vaguely alike, not that you could mistake one for the other, but I've wondered if they weren't the same person. They lived on the East Coast and were philosophical artists with a sensuous eye, committed to monolithic marriages. They both loved French culture and were self-mocking fellows who saw themselves as comedians, entranced by silence and ghostly presences. Of the sea, Stevens writes, "Like a body wholly body, fluttering / its empty sleeves." "Wholly" puns on "holy." He is saying thus, in accord with the greatest philosopher, that God is immanent, and whatever is *isn't* all there is, for there is everywhere only the weight and particular density of ubiquitous nothingness. The nothing that is always not there.

Hopper says that, too, particularly in his lighthouses, stark visionary towers at the edge of the sea, standing sightless in sunlight, full of dark seeing. Here, seeing puns on "sea." Stevens talks of singing beyond what you hear. Hopper's Eurydice, in her elegant shoes, thinks of Orpheus, hero of song, who fails to save her from Hades. His story is horribly sad. Orpheus's singing could enchant trees and birds, but no artist can save Eurydice. Had Orpheus saved her, he'd have made an end to desire, an end to art. His fate was to be torn to pieces by a horde of mythical women, naturally, who then flung his head into the ocean. It continues singing as it floats toward the island of Lesbos.

Eurydice feels guilty. She must tell Orpheus that she went to the party alone and met a man. Orpheus will want to know everything, and he'll never stop asking questions. This was in the old days when there was jealousy and infidelity. He'll cry. He'll say they can't be together anymore, but she knows he won't leave her.

Now against her hip Eurydice holds a flashlight to light the way into the sumptuous and fiery vault of the movie theater. Only a man and a woman are seen seated within watching the movie, close to each other but not seated together. They look lonely. The movie has been on for a while. Many seats remain empty. In Hopper's day, people often arrived in the middle of movies, which led to the expression you no longer hear, "This is where I came in."

The man and the woman who are not together make the theater seem to loom all about, luxuriously overwrought, the ceiling aglow with bulging red lights. They look like nipples suspended over the red seats. In its luxurious excess, the theater seems hollow, the space wasted. A column of thick, massively involved carving stands between the people and Eurydice. It has the look of lacerated, bleeding meat, but you hardy notice it at first. Eurydice doesn't notice it at all, doesn't realize it is the body of Orpheus.

But who can tell what she notices? The way her head is turned, she may be willfully ignoring the column. She may be petulant. Orpheus failed to save her. He got torn to pieces and she remained here, trapped in this dull usherette job, wearing a uniform. It looks very good on her, but she wants to put on her dress and go to the party.

Orpheus's head is singing while poor Eurydice, without a song

of her own, dreams of being saved from the lush and funereal theater, built for the primal drama of sacrifice, for fire and blood.
Ghosts play indistinctly on the blue, distant screen. A guilty red line
runs down the trouser leg of Eurydice's uniform. The bloody line
makes her connection to the theater both formal and metaphorical.
Formally, the theater is her workplace. Metaphorically, it is her
body, an interior darkness of desire and fantasy. She stands below
red shaded lamps that cast intense light, catching the edges of her
hair, giving morbid whiteness to her temple and wrist. Perhaps the
tendency of her thoughts is grim, like the woman's thoughts in
Stevens's poem "Sunday Morning," published fifteen years before
Hopper finished his painting. In the poem's sensuous setting, a
woman thinks of desire and sacrifice, and she wonders, "Why
should she give her bounty to the dead?" Her sister, Eurydice, the
uniformed girl, might ask the same question.

I heard voices in the adjoining gallery. My trance was broken. I
left quickly, as though I'd been discovered standing too close to
Eurydice, like the gangsterish man. But she heard no voices. She is
thinking, and hears nothing. People used to think. There used to
be silence, solitude, thinking. Hopper was known for just these
things, living half the year in semi-isolation on Cape Cod, where
he made paintings about the drama of thinking. That was half a
century ago. We no longer care about history, but from Hopper's
paintings you are reminded of what thinking felt like. In one painting, a fully clothed man sits on the edge of the bed, his back to the
naked bottom of a woman. She sleeps. Of her nakedness, he is
oblivious. He is thinking. The wife of the philosopher Heidegger
said to unwelcome visitors, "He is thinking." Heidegger wrote a
monograph titled "What Is Called Thinking" and spent his life
thinking about thinking. In another Hopper painting, a fully

clothed woman sits at the edge of a bed, her back to a naked man. His nakedness means nothing to her. She is thinking. Wearing clothes, apparently, makes thinking a personal experience, unlike nakedness, which is associated with impersonal, instinctive life. Today we are mad about nakedness. Some artists say, when working from live models, you must wait until they stop thinking. Thinking violates our obsession with surfaces. Totally white and totally black paintings hang in our museums while outside, wherever you look, graffiti attack surfaces. Names scream from walls, demanding recognition. There used to be selves before there were surfaces.

Eurydice couldn't be less naked, wearing a uniform, immersed in her thinking self. The great critic Friedrich Nietzsche might say she is an Apollonian figure in a Dionysian setting. Many theaters are called the Apollo. The best known, which is in Harlem, becomes Dionysian when an entertainer fails to charm the crowd.

Eurydice stands tightly contained in her blue uniform, and all about are the wild forms and colors of the theater, where instinctive life is made sensuous and dramatic. People used to say "naked passion" or "raw emotion" in praise of movies. It is the very thing you see in the Orphic column of the painting, so violently carved, bleeding. Stevens writes, "To lay his brain upon the board / And pick the acrid colors out." He means you can tear off Orpheus's head, but you can't see the singing.

I could have taken the subway downtown to Sheridan Square, a few blocks from Hopper's movie. Eurydice had left years earlier, in 1939, to stand in *New York Movie*, the year of the Hitler-Stalin pact, the year Poland was invaded. She belongs to a moment in history, like the appointments of the theater. The theater and Eurydice are properties of time. There used to be time. Guys would say they "made time" with a girl. There used to be girls. Now there's just guys, and there is nothing like time in the rage and blare of movies. There used to be plenty of time. There used to be day and night, and there was even a song called "Night and Day," which is very different from "A Hard Day's Night." In the thirties, forties, and fifties there was day and there was night. In Genesis, God separates the light from the darkness. He calls the light "Day." He calls the darkness "Night."

Hopper put the feeling of the hours into his paintings, the embrace of their shadows at night, their peculiar stillness in the afternoon, the different qualities of daylight, the quality of night. He painted a woman sitting up in bed as sunlight comes through a window, and a woman standing naked before a window. People used to look out of windows. The woman is naked but full of seeing, and not for us to gape at. There used to be obscenity. There used to be a distinction, as between day and night, between private and public. There used to be privacy. In Hopper's painting, the light calls the woman to look, to see the moment of the day, the time. Time is real, according to the philosopher Henri Bergson. He means organic rather than abstract. He means time is part of creation, and existed long before we put time into clocks. Bergson, who died in Nazi-occupied Paris, was contemporary with Hopper, and an influence on Stevens. What Hopper sees, Bergson means.

Hopper's usherette is adrift in her private thoughts, in the medium of real time, not the manufactured time of movies. There used to be real time and solitude and stillness. There used to be individuals, Apollonians, as well as the Dionysian public. Politicians used to say "Americans," which implies individuals, but they now say "the American people." No president now says to the American people, as Roosevelt used to say, "you and I know." A body was once the reality of a soul. "I love you body and soul," said the popular song, as if persons had an inner and outer aspect. The little word "and" seems pathetic, a banal insistence on wholeness. Hopper didn't worry about words. He discovered wholeness in silence, a painted moment of silence and stillness, either indoors or in the silent light of nature. Nighttime in Hopper's paintings can seem darkly luminous, or strangely theatrical, noir movie–like, a sensuous and enveloping darkness, alluring and scary, as if there is something out there that can't be dispelled by electricity.

Hopper loved movies. They influenced his work, and movies have paid tribute to Hopper. His *New York Movie* theater is the eye of darkness. His people are sometimes seen through windows at night, from the point of view of darkness, or they are seen just outside the house, as if they want to savor the ancient light. There used to be inner and outer, indoors and outdoors, you and nature. There used to be nature. People left the house to be within its light. There used to be light.

Published in *Vogue* and in *Edward Hopper and the American Imagination* (Whitney Museum of American Art/W. W. Norton, 1995).

II.

autobiographical essays

to feel these things

MY MOTHER, Anna Czeskies, was seventeen when she married and said good-bye to her parents in Brest Litovsk. She sailed to New York, settled in Coney Island, and moved later to a tenement in Manhattan, near my father's barbershop. Soon afterward, the year Hitler came to power and Roosevelt became president, I was born. These names, intoned throughout my childhood, belonged to mythical deities. One was evil. The other was the other.

My mother's family intended to follow her to America, but the day my grandfather went to get their emigration papers there was a pogrom. He was attacked in the street by a mob and left for dead. He didn't recover quickly. Then it was too late to get out of Poland.

In photos he is pale and thin. Skin pulls tight across sharp bones in a narrow face. He has the alert, hypersensitive look of an ill-nourished person, but sits correctly, posing old-style, as if a photo is serious business. He was a tailor who made uniforms for Polish army officers, and he had a feeling for posture. My mother says they threw his unconscious body into a cellar. I heard the story around the time children hear fairy tales. Once upon a time my grandfather was walking in the street . . .

Years later I would hear that organized terrorism had been reported for centuries in Europe, Russia, and the Middle East. Rabbinical commentaries engaged questions as to whether the community should surrender a few to save the rest, die with the few, or resist. Rabbis consulted the commentaries while the SS prepared gas chambers and worked out train schedules. When the Nazis seized Brest Litovsk, my grandfather, grandmother, and their youngest daughter, my mother's sister, were buried in a pit with others.

As my mother sat in the living room at night, waiting for my father to come home from work, she sometimes cried. This was my personal experience of the Holocaust, in a three-room apartment on the Lower East Side of Manhattan, amid claw-footed furniture covered by plastic to protect the fabric.

I had no concrete understanding of her grief. I'd never met my grandparents, uncles, or aunt. I had to imagine things—the story about my grandfather, the danger of the streets. Eventually, I figured it was bad for Jews the way *it* is said to be raining. I didn't know what *it* was, only that *it* was worse than Hitler, older, absolutely unreasonable, strong, able to do things like fix the plumbing and paint the walls. *It* was like animals and trees, what lives outside, more physical than a person, though *it* appeared in persons. With this understanding, I was slow to perform simple childhood actions—riding a bicycle, throwing a ball, running like other bodies—that expressed one's being-at-home-in-the-world.

My mother—without parents, siblings, friends, or English— was generally intimidated by America, even fearful of going out alone in the streets. She had black hair, which she wore in long braids. Her eyes were blue. Strange men wanted to approach and talk to her. She kept me close. We were constantly together. Her many fears nourished mine, especially because I was sickly, susceptible to respiratory diseases and ear infections—colds, bronchitis, pleurisy, and pneumonia twice. Through feverish delirium, I heard my mother at my bedside saying, *"Meir far deir,"* which means "Let me die rather than you." Her phrase, repeated like a radio signal, kept me from drifting out of life.

I learned English mainly from the woman who lived next door. Her name was Lynn Nations. She came from Texas and was married to a Jew, Arthur Kleinman, a furrier and lefty intellectual. They had no children. She worked at Saks Fifth Avenue, a tall, slender woman with fine features and light brown hair. She was proud of her legs, and she flaunted a tough, classy manner. I remember the clack of her high heels on the marble floor of the outside hallway. I was often in her apartment and she in ours, telling us the smart things she'd said that day at Saks, how she corrected her customers' taste and sold them half the store. We understood her idea of herself, if not always what she said, but she talked at us for years, teasing us toward English. To her, my Yiddish was hilarious. "Arthur, did you hear what he called the telephone wire? A *shtrik*. No wonder he's afraid of it."

Arthur, fluent in Yiddish, looked at me in astonishment. *"Das iz nisht a shtrik. Das iz a telephone vyeh."* I see his Slavic face leaning down, thick in nose and lip, winking at me, compromising English and Yiddish to assure me that meaning is greater than words.

When I came crying from the playground after some kid hit me, Lynn's eyes contracted into icy dots of rage. She snatched me from my mother by the back of my neck—"You let go of your child"—and steered me into the playground and thrust me toward the kid. Still crying, I started swinging, and it was good, it was excellent, for a scrawny, sickly kid to hear his blubbering become curses and to be a piece of nature in a playground fistfight. Lynn hated my crying, seeing it as pogrom-obsessed *Yiddishkeit*. For her better opinion, I made small beginnings, used my fists, spoke English. During the war I changed further.

I put a big map of Europe on my bedroom wall. When I read about Allied bombing raids in Germany, Italy, or elsewhere, I found the city and stuck a red pin into it. I imagined myself a B-17 pilot or bombardier. In movies, I saw the doors of the bomb bay swing open and long bombs with tails and sticklike incendiaries fall away toward factories, railroad tracks, and whole cities. This great work was being done by regular guys from America. My mother took me to the movies on Friday afternoons after school. Before we left, I had to drink a glass of milk. I hated its whiteness, the whiteness of its taste. "Finish the whole glass. It's good for you." But then came the B-17, struck with machine guns in ribs, nose, belly, and tail, a primordial reptile dragging long flaps and lugubrious claws for landing gear, lumbering up into the gray dawn among its thousand sisters, each bearing a sacred gift of bombs.

After the war, her brothers' names appeared in the *Forward*, published a few blocks from us, in a white building opposite the Seward Park Library that I'd passed many times on the way to my father's barbershop around the corner on Henry Street. The distant, the exotic, the fairy tale of evil and a murdered family was suddenly in these familiar streets, even in the Garden Cafeteria near the foot of the *Forward* building, where I sometimes sat with my father and ate whitefish on black bread with onion, amid the dark Jewish faces of taxi drivers, pickle salesmen, dry-goods merchants, journalists, and other urban beings who sipped coffee or borscht, smoked cigarettes, argued, joked, or complained in Yiddish, or in such English as had been mutilated into the nuances required by Yiddish, grammatical niceties flung aside so that meaning and feeling could walk on the earth.

The names of my uncles, Yussel and Srulke Czeskies, had appeared among those of survivors gathered in camps for displaced persons who now sought relations in America. One uncle had been in the Russian army, the other in the Polish army. I was happy. I was also worried. Would my mother be held responsible for what they had endured? When her brother Srulke actually stood in our apartment, I retreated to corners, absorbed in shadowy thoughts, like a neighborhood cat. A strange mechanism of feeling drew me from happiness toward internal complications; early notions of guilt as fundamental to life.

The father of a friend of mine developed his own religious practices, reducing life to secret study and his tuxedo-renting business. He was a big gloomy man with a high rounded back, black brows, and a reproachful glare. During the day, he worked. At night, he studied. He sought the deepest meaning of things, the fate of the Jews. There had been a tragic mistake. He would discover, in holy books, how to understand the Holocaust.

Even as a child, I thought Jews were obsessed with meaning. We didn't just eat, sleep, work, study, and play, but needed the meaning of these things and everything. Meaning as such, as if it had practical value, like wood or gold. We sought it with brain fingers, loved how it feels in the elaborations of talk. At the heart of all meaning was religion, the law, forever established yet open to perpetual analysis and explication. But I knew that beneath all meaning was the general complicity with murder. In the sidewalks, the grass, the weather, and the human heart: the need to murder.

And yet, outside, in murderous nature, I could see that colors never clash and that the world is everywhere beautiful. I feared its allure.

I remember pictures of President Roosevelt, the long, handsome face with its insouciant smile, the cigarette holder aloft in a white aristocratic hand, perhaps in the manner of SS officers chatting and smoking outside the windows of the gas chambers as we died in agony visible to them. Of course, I wasn't there. I had only a sense of ubiquitous savagery, the inchoate, nightmarish apprehensions of a child, much like insanity or the numinousness of a religious vision where ideas have the force of presence, overriding logic. Yiddish-speaking relatives discussed the President's tepid reaction to Kristallnacht and his decision to turn away a ship of Jewish refugees from American shores. From those who could make a difference, I figured, came indifference. Knowing nothing about immigration laws and isolationist politics of America, I understood only a weird mixture of comfort and sadism in the President's smile. In his capacity to do something lived the frisson of doing nothing. I couldn't have articulated this understanding any more than I could have said how I untie my shoelaces.

"Take care," writes Primo Levi, "not to suffer in your own homes what is inflicted on us here." He means don't let his experience of Auschwitz become yours. I read the sentence repeatedly before I understood that is all he means, and that he doesn't mean: DON'T FEEL THESE THINGS IN THE DAILINESS OF YOUR LIFE OR IT WILL POISON EVERYTHING ELSE—running in the playground, speaking English, knowing it's time to make a fist.

Thus, misreading a few words, I rediscover my primitive apprehensions long after the Holocaust. I literally remind myself that I wasn't with my grandparents in Poland, or with the children packed into cattle trains to the death camps. I can't claim too little. Nothing happened to me. I was a sickly kid, burdened by sweaters and scarves and winter coats buttoned to the neck. If I loosened my scarf or undid a coat button, my mother would fly into a state of panic, as though millions of germs were shooting through the gap I'd made in my clothing.

The original version of this essay was published in *Testimony: Contemporary Writers Make the Holocaust Personal*, edited by David Rosenberg (Times Books, 1989). Later, it was rewritten in its current form in *To Feel These Things* (Mercury House, 1993).

the zipper

A man goes to bed with Gilda and wakes up with me.
—RITA HAYWORTH *(born Margarita Carmen Cansino, 1918)*

My mistress' eyes are nothing like the sun.
—WILLIAM SHAKESPEARE

RITA HAYWORTH stars in *Gilda*, but she isn't seen for the first fif-teen minutes while the friendship of two men, played by George Macready and Glenn Ford, is established. Macready saves Ford from being robbed on the docks of Buenos Aires, then hires Ford to manage a gambling casino owned by Macready. They become trusting, affectionate pals in a nightlife society where women are marginal. Then Macready leaves on a business trip to the "interior." When Macready returns, Ford hurries to Macready's mansion and is surprised to hear about a woman whom Macready just met and married. The woman is heard singing, a muted voice in the interior distance, in a bedroom, in the depths of Macready's mansion. Macready leads Ford toward the singing, into the bedroom, to meet the woman, and—cut—Rita Hayworth lifts her face to look into the camera and see who is there. In this gesture, with all the magic of the word, Rita Hayworth "appears." She is bathed in light, seems even to exude it like a personal quality, like her wavy hair, her voice, and the flow of her body when walking or dancing.

She looks into the camera, into me, my interior, and I see that the friendship of Macready and Ford is in trouble, for this is the beautiful face of betrayal, jealousy, murder, suicide, war. It is the face of love from Homer to Shakespeare to the nineteen forties.

Like other actresses of her day, Rita Hayworth had mythic power and could carry a movie without a male star. I thought she carried *Gilda* despite George Macready and Glenn Ford. In my view, they were of slightly repulsive dramatic interest, but I was about thirteen when I saw the movie. I took it as seriously as life. How could Rita Hayworth get involved with guys like that?

Macready, playing a Nazi agent who lives in Argentina, walks rigidly erect, carrying a sword cane. He looks frosty, pockmarked, and desiccated, like the surface of the moon. There is something priestly about him, a lofty, ascetic air. Ford, playing a low-life hustler who cheats at cards and dice, has a soft, dark, sensuous look, sensitive rather than intelligent. He smiles and wiggles around Macready in a flirty way. Wiggly and Rigid form a love triangle with Rita Hayworth, very degrading to her, since she is way out of their league, but then she is repeatedly humiliated in the movie. She seems to ask for it, even to need it badly; once, she actually crawls at Ford's feet. Humiliation, essential plot matter in Hollywood and novels, is probably basic to fiction generally. Even the cherished *Alice in Wonderland* has to do with humiliation: a girl falls into a hole and is then repeatedly insulted in mind and body. When I saw *Gilda*, I didn't wonder if there was a universal need for such subterranean experience.

Much dramatic tension is created when neither Rita Hayworth nor Ford tells Macready—who is made suspicious by their instantaneous, mutual hostility—that they already know each other and were once lovers. By not telling Macready, they betray him. Ford thinks he is loyal to Macready, protecting his peace of mind, etc., and he is angry at the intrusion of Rita Hayworth into his paradisal friendship. He says, in a voice-over after Macready presents him to her, that he wanted to hit her, and he also wanted to hit Macready. Ford is bitterly frustrated and confused. I disliked him, but I suffered his anguish.

Trying not to succumb to Rita Hayworth's charms, Ford becomes increasingly self-righteous and more rigid than Macready. There is an excruciating moment when Macready, concerned not to look like a jealous husband, tells Ford to pull Rita Hayworth away as she dances with another man in Macready's casino. But she will not only dance with other men, she will also go out with them. She doesn't love Macready; she fears him, and yet she makes him jealous of Ford, just as she makes Ford jealous of her and other men. It emerges that her licentious bitchery means only that she loves Ford; he loves her, too. They are trapped in a viciously delicious game of mutual detestation that becomes the main plot. It complicates, in a feminine way, through flamboyant gestures and shows of feeling. The subplot, full of male violence—guns, fistfights, crime, war—is turgid and easy to forget. You might say the movie is sexually structured, the woman (feeling) on top.

Rita Hayworth, with her amazing blond light in this dark movie (where almost everything happens in rooms, and even the outdoors seem indoors), suggests that dark and light are Manichaean opposites: dark is evil; light is good. Gray represents confusion of good and evil. I certainly didn't have this thought when I saw the movie in the Loews theater on Canal Street, on the Lower East Side of Manhattan. I didn't think anything. I felt the meaning of things, especially the morally murky weight of the gray-lighted bedroom scene where Rita Hayworth asks Macready to unzip her dress as she lies on a bed. She says more than once that she has trouble with zippers, a helpless girl imprisoned in the dress of a grown-up. Zippers, a major erotic trope of forties movies, represented a man's access to a woman's body, despite its metal teeth.

I didn't want Macready to unzipper Rita Hayworth's dress. I didn't want Macready to touch her, though she is married to him, and she herself invites physical intimacy. Macready has told Ford he is "crazy about her," so his heart is in the right place. Nevertheless, I didn't want him to touch Rita Hayworth. He didn't really love her; didn't even feel desire or lust, only a sickening idea of possession and a mysterious need for betrayal. Why else would he hire Ford, a known cheater, as his most trusted assistant? And why else would Macready marry a woman—even Rita Hayworth—he has known only one day?

Macready flaunts his frightening sword cane, which he calls his "friend," but he moves in a delirium of masochistic self-destruction, and he is finally stabbed in the back by his "friend," literally the cane, metaphorically Ford. Macready gets what he deserves, which is what he wants, including sexual betrayal by Ford. Despite Ford's furious resistance to her, Ford gets Rita Hayworth, which is what she wants. Everything seems to work out, to balance and close, but not for me. I left the movie haunted by images of Rita Hayworth, yearning for her.

She had so much beauty and vitality that I assumed she would recover from what Macready did after unzippering her dress. Whatever it was, it wasn't good, but I supposed it happened a lot in Hollywood, where men go about touching women without feeling love, and—utterly unbearable—there are women who want to be

Macreadied. Thus: in the religioso movie darkness, I saw Rita Hayworth request her own humiliation by the ascetic, priestly, frightening Macready. Zip. She is sacrificed and apotheosized. I had to remind myself that *Gilda* is a movie, not real life, and George Macready is a fine actor; also, probably, a nice guy.

No use.

The creep touched her.

I understood that real life is this way.

Nothing would be the same for me again.

I wanted to forget the scene, but it had happened as if to me, and was now fixed in my personal history more indelibly than World War II. Only an instant of zipper business, yet it colored my love for Rita Hayworth with pity and grief. She lay there, utterly still and vulnerable, and Macready leaned over her the way kids play doctor, an eerily erotic game.

Seeing this was like a criminal privilege, though I was only sitting in a movie theater, doing nothing but looking. But I looked. I didn't shut my eyes. Unspeakable apprehensions—pleasure?—were aroused in me, in my head or heart, that secret, interior, moral theater (as opposed to the public showplace, the Loews Canal) where movies dreamily transpire, differently for each of us. I disapproved of the sensations, the so-called pleasure, but pleasure and disapproval feed on each other. Rita Hayworth will be all right in the morning, I told myself. It won't matter what Macready did, though it was shameful and sad. What I felt was, perhaps, felt by millions.

Today, these feelings are considered sentimental, quaint. They have lost force and spontaneity. We still have them, maybe, but they no longer have us. Macready did it to Rita Hayworth. So? He didn't rape her. The scene ended. I didn't have to watch Macready actually do anything, not that it would have been possible to film

Macready in bed, doing things to Rita Hayworth, without destroy-
ing the movie. The remake of *Gilda* will, of course, show Macready
doing everything, but it must be remembered that *Gilda* was
released when feelings—like clothing styles, popular dances, car
designs—were appreciated differently from today. Perhaps feelings
as such had a far higher value. Movies didn't have to show naked
bodies, fucking, paraphilia, or graphic mutilation and bloody
murder. Techniques of suggestion were cultivated—the zipper, for
example—and less was more except in regard to words. There were
long scenes brilliant with words. We didn't so much use our eyes,
like roots digging into visible physical bodies for the nourishment
of meanest sensation. The ear, more sensuous than sensual, received
the interior life of people, as opposed to what is sucked up by the
salacious eyeball.

Later in the movie, Rita Hayworth asks again for help with her
zipper, during a nightclub routine, as she does a striptease dance.
Several men hurry to oblige and help her become naked. Ford
notices, has a tizzy, stops things from going too far. He slaps her.
His hand doesn't wither and rot. Not only is there injustice, there is
no justice. I feel so sorry for her, not to mention myself, poor kid,
having to grow up, to know such things. Rita Hayworth is never
seen disrobed in the movie, though it is threatened more than once.
The atmosphere of dark repression and mysterious forces—the
mood or feeling of the movie—might be destroyed by the revelation of her body. It scared me as she began her striptease dance in
the nightclub. I didn't want everybody to see her body, or even to
see that Rita Hayworth had a body. (The length of her beautiful
left leg is fleetingly exposed by a slit in her dress as she dances.)

Two years later, I had sex for the first time, and I was taken by
a weird sorrow riding home alone in the subway, as visceral odors

lifted from my hands, reminding me that I'd fallen a few hours ago with my girlfriend—both of us virgins—from Heights of Desire, into bodies. (Religious movements, West and East, have cultivated a practice of dreamily disembodied, extended, nonorgasmic sex, as described in John Donne's poem "The Ecstasy.")

In plain sight of Ford, who is obliged by his job to watch her, Rita Hayworth flirts with other men and says, "If I were a ranch, they'd call me the Bar Nothing." She thus tortures Ford, showing him—in the desires of other men—the body he can't let himself have. Ford watches. He tries to seem angry, then blurts out that Rita Hayworth can do whatever she pleases. It doesn't matter to him. He says he will personally deliver Rita Hayworth to her other men, then pick her up like "laundry" and return her to Macready. In effect, everything Rita Hayworth does with other men will be determined and controlled by Ford. Impassioned and irrational, Ford doesn't know what he means.

My moral notions, already disturbed, were further disturbed: the hero talks like this? I was being introduced to deep stuff, subterranean forces, years before I understood what was happening to me, or maybe the world in the forties. It had to do with sex— hardly anything doesn't—but I didn't know about sex. I believed something more important was at stake. I saw Bad presenting itself—in the form of pleasure—as entertainment, and I was being made to know that I was susceptible to the pleasure of Bad, if for no other reason than that Bad was in me, like Gog and Magog.

Was the experience indeed pleasure, not merely a strong sensation, like the electric excitement of an idea, or the effect of a novelty, or a demonic, masturbatory fantasy? If it was a real feeling, could I be violated by it, my own real feeling? Could it happen to anyone? If so, could anyone ever be a good person?

I continued to wonder—without words to analyze or describe it—about the distinction, in real life, between pleasure and its innumerable imitations. Saint Augustine says, "the love of this world is fornication against God," and that's that. For me, the question was: If I felt something I believed was bad, but it felt good, would I want to fornicate against God again and again? And would I then despise other pleasures, assuming other pleasures remained to me? Had Macready unzipped me, too? In Flannery O'Connor's masterpiece "A Good Man Is Hard to Find," a mystical murderer says, "It's no real pleasure in life." I wondered about real pleasure. What is it?

Ford's antiheroic, homoerotic hysteria, basic to the dramatic effect in *Gilda*, is virtually explicit when Rita Hayworth suggests that a psychiatrist can tell Ford that he likes the idea of Rita Hayworth as "laundry," or dirty—that is, of her doing things with other men. I didn't understand this in feeling or thought. Is sexual infidelity—deserving of death in the colorful Mediterranean community where I lived—what Ford likes? I didn't see his angry, tyrannical show of controlling power as a refusal to acknowledge that he is the hapless creature of dark impulsions. Rita Hayworth understands what's going on in Ford, but Ford never gains understanding of himself. Instead, he becomes sadistically determined to punish Rita Hayworth for his inadmissible need to see her do what he likes her to do.

Gilda—written by a woman, starring a woman, produced by a woman—suggests that women know better than men what men are looking at when men look at women. They know that such looking—a function of blindness—is not seeing. In effect, Rita Hayworth exists fantastically for Macready and Ford within the so-called male gaze. She is created by their looking, a form of ideolog-

ical hypnosis, or blindness, or stupidity, perhaps crucial to the per-
petuation of human society as it now exists. In the movie, the male
gaze keeps two men fixated on a woman rather than each other.
Outside the movie, in real life, Rita Hayworth was the fixation of
millions of men in the armed services, their favorite pinup girl. An
erotic icon, she kept our boys straight.

In *Gilda*, Rita Hayworth famously sings one song several times.
(I later found out her voice is dubbed; also, her hair is dyed, her
hairline is fake, her name is Margarita.) The refrain of her song is
"Put the blame on Mame, boys." Mame (Freudian pun intended) is
responsible for cataclysmic occurrences—the Chicago fire, a terrible snowstorm, etc. (She's hot, the city burns; she's cold, "for seven
days they shoveled snow.") The song ironically implies that boys,
who are exquisitely tortured by her capricious dominatrixiness,
want to imagine that Mame has tremendous, annihilating power. I
could see the amusement in Rita Hayworth's eyes as she pretends to
sing, and I loved her for that, her peculiar quality of spirit. Not
quite playing the role, she is more real, nearly accessible, more
heartbreaking.

The audience learns that Ford abandoned her in the "interior"
when he ran out of money, before the movie begins. To express the
audience's contempt for him, the attendant in the men's room of
Macready's gambling casino, a comic philosophical figure, lowly
and godlike, twice calls Ford a "peasant." Ford lacks aristocratic
sensibility, or class. But Rita Hayworth gives him an opportunity to
transcend himself by choosing her over his career as Macready's
thing. He doesn't choose her until the end of the movie, when he
supposes Macready is dead. Ford thus remains a peasant, or, at best,
a grubby careerist who takes his work more seriously than love.

The movie ends. Poor Rita Hayworth goes off with Ford. A winter night, streetlights, traffic—the shock of the real—awaited me.

I went down Madison Street, passing under the Manhattan Bridge, then turning left on Market Street, walking toward the East River, until I came to Monroe Street and turned right. These directions, these streets, restored me to my life. I passed the tenements with their Italian grocery stores and candy stores, and I passed my old elementary school, P.S. 177, a huge, grim, soot-dark Victorian building. From the Church of Saint Joseph, at the corner of Catherine and Monroe streets, I heard a bell tolling the hour. The church stood opposite our second-floor apartment in a building called Knickerbocker Village. Walking down Monroe Street, I approached the wavering light of Friday-night prayer candles in our kitchen window. The shadow of my mother, against the window shade, moved from refrigerator to stove. Everything as it should be. Italian ladies with shopping bags and baby carriages. Italian kids sitting on the stoops of their tenements. This was real. Too different—like a blond woman who might bring the solidity and value of this neighborhood into question—wasn't good.

The darkness of the movie, like a darkness inside me, contained nothing real, but there was a faint glow of *Gilda* within it, and I felt tumultuous yearning for Rita Hayworth—the woman, not the actress. I yearned to bring her home, where she would descend, or lovingly condescend, to sweet reconciliation with the ordinariness of my life, even its banality and boredom, which I believed was good. The good. My mother, cooking good dinner in the small but good kitchen of our three-room apartment, would be embarrassed. She would apologize to bad Rita Hayworth for not having prepared a more sumptuous dinner, but I hadn't given any warning.

"Do you like borscht? It's good. Do you know, Miss Hayworth, the good doctor who delivered your bad baby is my good cousin from Canada? When he told me that he delivered your bad baby, I almost fainted. Maybe you remember him. Tall. Curly hair."

It was like this for me, in a day when love, even the terrible anguish it was known to inflict, was praised and much desired. As for Rita Hayworth—dream of heroes, three husbands, millions of servicemen—she was love, catastrophic, wild, impossible to domesticate. So much of her life was public, spectacular imagery that it is hard to suppose she also had a real life, or to suppose that her feelings about Rita Hayworth were not the same as ours.

Originally published in *The Threepenny Review*, Summer 1991, and reprinted in *The Best American Essays of 1992*, edited by Susan Sontag, and in *To Feel These Things* (Mercury House, 1993).

literary talk

ABOUT FORTY YEARS AGO, in a high-school English class, I learned that talking about literature is like talking about yourself, except that literary talk is logical and polite, a social activity of nice people. My teacher's name was McLean, a thin man with a narrow head and badly scarred tissue about his mouth, which was obscured by a mustache, British and military-looking. The scar tissue was plain enough, despite the mustache, like crinkled wrapping paper with a pink sheen. Listening to him, looking at his face, I heard his voice as crushed; softly crushed by the grief around his mouth. He'd been in the air force. I suppose it happened during the war.

McLean usually wore an old brown tweed suit and a dull, appropriate tie, and he had a gentle, formal manner, nearly timid. Whenever he made some little joke, he chuckled nervously, as though he'd gone too far, exceeded the propriety of the classroom. Telling jokes calls attention to your mouth; his for sure. Some days, as if sensitive to weather, the scar tissue looked raw, hot, incompletely healed.

Long before McLean's class, I knew the strong effects of stories and poems, but through him I discovered you could talk about their effects as if they inhered in the words, just as his voice inhered in his face. When McLean read poetry aloud, his voice became vibrant, and the air of the classroom seemed full of pleasure, feeling its way into me with my breathing.

One afternoon, discussing *The Winter's Tale*, McLean came to a passage I didn't like. Paulina and Dion debate whether or not King Leontes should remarry. Years ago, deranged by evil jealousy, Leontes practically murdered his former queen, Hermione. Paulina says to Dion, "You are one of those / Would have him wed again." Dion replies:

> . . . *What were more holy*
> *Than to rejoice the former queen is well?*
> *What holier than . . .*
> *To bless the bed of majesty again*
> *With a sweet fellow to't?*

The queen is dead; long live the queen. All in all, Dion's speech imagines the dead queen alive, blessing "the bed of majesty again," in another woman's body, which will restore "a sweet fellow to't." The "to't," like a bird belching rather than tweeting, seemed to me disgusting, and Dion's whole speech, conflating a real dead woman and an imagined living one, was very creepy. I raised my hand. McLean looked at me. I said, "Necrophilia."

McLean asked me to stay after class, then went on, enraptured by the moment when Hermione steps out of the stone statue of herself and back into the living world. But I could only think that Leontes, much older now than the long-dead Hermione—their daughter being grown up and marriageable—can look forward to going to bed with Hermione once again, making love to her. Old Evil eating innocence, as in a black vision of Goya. Poor Hermione, tragically abused, would now be debauched by Leontes, criminal psychopath, her husband. I wouldn't accept the idea of her statue showing her as aged. Wouldn't see it. Couldn't.

After class, everyone left the room but McLean and me. I went up to his desk. He fooled with papers. He couldn't simply turn to me and say what was on his mind. Too direct. He collected papers, ordered them, collecting himself. I was scared. I was always scared. Not a good student, I didn't feel morally privileged to receive McLean's attention—alone, this close. It was hard for me even to raise my hand amid the pool of heads, then speak. I'd go deaf when McLean responded, and I'd sit nodding like a fool, understanding nothing, hearing nothing, the blood noisy in my head and my tie jumping to my heartbeat. Though barely perceptible, it could be seen.

Still looking at his papers, McLean said, "Some people make a practice of burying their dead quickly and getting on with life." My people, presumably. I didn't know why he said that, but I took the distinction without resentment. He was thinking out loud, unable to talk to me otherwise, perhaps too embarrassed by what he wanted to say, or his inability to say it. Then he said, "I was a ball-turret gunner." He was telling me a story.

Ball-turret gunners, in the belly of a B-17, the most vulnerable part, were frequently killed. McLean said he would become terrified in action. He'd spin and spin the turret, firing even when the German fighter planes were out of range. He gazed at me, but his eyes weren't engaging mine, perhaps seeing a vast and lethal sky, the earth whirling below in flames. On his last mission he was ordered to replace the side gunner of another B-17 who had been killed. It was the worst mission he'd ever flown. The B-17 was hit repeat-edly. It lost an engine, the landing gear was destroyed, and it was crashing on its belly. The man in the ball turret had to get out, but there was mangled steel above him. He couldn't move; he was trapped. As they went down, McLean bent over him. He looked up at McLean. "His eyes were big," said McLean. "Big."

I felt myself plummet through the dark well of my body. McLean's eyes were big, big. In that moment of utter horror, he whispered, "It's a great play, *The Winter's Tale*. Can you believe me?"

Published as "Literary Talk" in *The Threepenny Review*, Fall 1987, and reprinted in *To Feel These Things* (Mercury House, 1993).

my father

SIX DAYS A WEEK he rose early, dressed, ate breakfast alone, put on his hat, and walked to his barbershop at 207 Henry Street on the Lower East Side of Manhattan, about half a mile from our apartment. He returned after dark. The family ate dinner together on Sundays and Jewish holidays. Mainly he ate alone. I don't remember him staying home from work because of illness or bad weather. He took few vacations. Once we spent a week in Miami, and he tried to enjoy himself, wading bravely into the ocean, stepping inch by inch into the warm, blue, unpredictable immensity. Then he slipped. In water no higher than his *pupik*, he came up thrashing, struggling back onto the beach on skinny white legs. "I nearly drowned," he said, exhilarated. He never went into the water again. He preferred his barbershop to the natural world, retiring after thirty-five years, only when his hands trembled too much for scissors and razors and angina made it impossible for him to stand for hours at a time. Then he took walks in the neighborhood, carrying a vial of whiskey in his shirt pocket. When pain stopped him in the street, he'd stand very still and sip his whiskey. A few times I stood beside him, as still as he, waiting for the pain to end, both of us speechless and frightened.

He was vice president of his synagogue, keeping records, attending to the maintenance of the building. He spoke Yiddish, Polish, maybe some Russian, and the Hebrew necessary for prayers. He spoke to me in Yiddish until, at about the age of six, I began speaking to him mainly in English. When he switched from Yiddish to English, I'd rarely notice. He could play the violin and mandolin. As a youth in Poland, he'd been in a band. When old friends visited our apartment, he'd drink a schnapps with them. He smoked cigars and pipes. He read the Yiddish newspaper, the *Forward*, and the *Daily News*. He voted Democratic but had no faith in politicians, political systems, or "the people." Aside from family, work, and synagogue, his passion was friends. My mother reminded me, when I behaved badly, of his friends. She'd say, "Nobody will like you." Everybody liked Leon Michaels.

He was slightly more than five feet tall. My mother is barely five feet. Because I'm five nine, she thinks I'm a giant. My father came from Drohiczyn (Dro-hee-chin), a town on the river Bug near the Russian border. When I visited Poland in 1979, I asked my hosts about Drohiczyn. They said, "You'll see new buildings and Russian troops. No reason to go there." I didn't go there. It would have been a sentimental experience, essentially empty. My father never talked about the town, rarely said anything about his past. We also never had deep talks of the father-and-son kind. But when I was fifteen I fell in love, and he said a memorable thing to me.

The girl had many qualities—tall, blond, talented, musician—but mainly she wasn't Jewish. My father learned about her when we were seen together watching a basketball game at Madison Square Garden, among eighteen thousand people. I'd been foolish to suppose I could go to the Garden with a blonde and not be spotted. My father had many friends. You saw them in his barbershop, "the boys," snazzy dressers jingling coins in their pockets or poor Jews from the neighborhood who came just to sit, to rest in their passage between miseries. Always a crowd in the barbershop— cabdrivers, bookies, waiters, salesmen. One of them spotted me and phoned my father. When I returned that night, he was waiting up with that fact. He said we would discuss it in the morning.

I lay awake in anguish. No way to deny a girl I loved. I'd been seeing her secretly for months. Her parents knew about the secrecy. I was so ashamed of it that when I called for her, I'd ring the bell and then wait in the street. She urged me to come upstairs, meet her parents. After a while, I did. They understood. Her previous boyfriend was the son of a rabbi.

In the morning my father said, "Let's take a walk." We walked around the block, then around the block again, in silence. It took a long time, but the silence was so dense, it felt like one infinitely heavy immobilized minute. Then, as if he'd rehearsed a speech and dismissed it, he sighed. "I'll dance at your wedding."

Thus we spent a minute together, father and son, and he said a memorable thing. It is concise, its burden huge. If witty, it is so in the manner of Hieronymus Bosch, making a picture of demonic gaiety. My wedding takes place in the middle of the night. My father is a small figure among dancing Jews, frenzied with joy.

For a fifteen-year-old in love, this sentence was a judgment, punishment, and release from a brutal sanction. He didn't order me not to see her. I could do as I pleased. As it happened, she met someone else and broke up with me. I was very hurt. I was also relieved. My father danced at my wedding, twelve years later, when I married Sylvia. Black-haired. Dark-skinned. Jew. Because her parents were dead, the ceremony was held in our apartment. Her aunts and uncles sat along the wall, mine along another. The living room was small. Conversation, forced by closeness, was lively and nervous. The rabbi, delayed by traffic, arrived late, and the ceremony was hurried. Everyone seemed to shout instructions. Did she circle me or I her? My father was delighted. When Sylvia and I fought, which was every day, she'd sometimes threaten to tell my father the truth about me. "It will kill him," she said.

I'd tried once to talk to him about our trouble. He wouldn't hear it. "She's an orphan. You cannot abandon her."

If he ever hit me, I don't remember it, but I remember being malicious. My brother, three years younger than I, was practicing scales on my father's violin. When he finished, he started to carry the violin across the room. I put out my foot. He tripped, fell. We heard the violin hit the floor and crack. Quicker than instantly, I wanted to undo the act, not trip my brother. But it was done. I was stuck with myself. I think I smiled. My father looked at the violin and said, "I had it over twenty years."

Maybe I tripped my brother because I'm tone-deaf. I can't learn to play a musical instrument. Nothing forgives me. I wish my father had become enraged, knocked off my head, so I could forget the incident. I never felt insufficiently loved, and yet I think: When Abraham raised the knife to Isaac, the kid had it good.

In photos, however badly lit or ill-focused, my father looks like himself. I never look like myself. This isn't me, I think. Like a baby, my father is inevitably himself.

My father never owned a car or flew in an airplane. He imagined no alternatives to being himself. He had his family, his friends, his neighborhood, synagogue, and the hectic variety of human traffic in the barbershop and the streets. Looking out my window

above San Francisco Bay, I think how my father saw only Monro
Street, Madison Street, and Clinton Street. For thirty-five years, he
walked to work.

I was in London, returning from three months in Paris, when
he died. My flight to New York had been canceled. I was stranded,
waiting for another flight. Nobody in New York knew where I
was. I couldn't be phoned. The day after the funeral, I arrived. My
brother met me at the door of the apartment and told me the news.
I went alone to my parents' bedroom and sat on the bed. I didn't
want to be seen crying.

A great number of people visited the apartment to offer condo-
lences and to reminisce. Then a rabbi came, a tiny, fragile man
dressed in black, with a white beard twice the length of his face. It
looked like the top of his shirt. He asked my mother to give him
some of my father's clothes, particularly things he'd worn next to
his skin, because he was a good man, very rare. As the rabbi started
to leave with a bundle of clothes in his arms, he noticed me sitting
at the kitchen table. He said in Yiddish, "Sit lower."

I didn't know what he was getting at. Did he want me to
crouch? I was somehow susceptible to criticism.

My mother interceded. "He feels," she said. "He feels plenty."

"I didn't ask him how he feels. Tell him to sit lower."

I got up and left the kitchen, looking for a lower place to sit. I
was very angry but not enough to start yelling at a fanatical midget.
Besides, he was correct.

ONE FRIDAY NIGHT, I was walking to the subway on Madison
Street. My winter coat was open, flying with my stride. I wore a
white shirt and a sharp red tie. I'd combed my hair in the style of the

day, a glorious pompadour fixed and sealed with Vaseline. I was nineteen-years-old terrific. The night was cold, but I was hot. The wind was strong. My hair was stronger. It gleamed like a black, polished rock. As I entered the darkness below the Manhattan Bridge, where it strikes across Madison Street and makes a high, gloomy, mysterious vault, I met my father. He was returning from the barbershop, following his usual route. His coat was buttoned to his chin, his hat pulled down to protect his eyes. He stopped. As I approached him, I saw him study me, his creation. We stood for a moment beneath the bridge, facing each other in the darkness and wind. An American giant, five feet nine inches tall. A short Polish Jew. He said, "Button your coat. Everybody doesn't have to see your tie."

I buttoned my coat.

"Why don't you wear a hat?"

I sighed. "I'm all right."

"You need a haircut. You look like a bum."

"I'll come to the barbershop tomorrow."

He nodded, as if to say "Good night" and "What's the use." He was on his way home to dinner, to sleep. He'd worked all day. I was on my way to sexual adventure. Then he asked, "Do you need money?"

"No."

"Here," he said, pulling coins from his coat pocket. "For the subway. Take."

He gave.

I took.

This essay was originally published as "My Father's Life" in *Esquire*, October 1981; then in *The Granta Book of the Family*, edited by Bill Buford (Granta Books, 1995); and later in its current form as "My Father" in *Shuffle* (Farrar, Straus and Giroux, 1990).

the abandoned
house

I LIVED WITH TWO OTHER GRADUATE STUDENTS, Jay Norden
and David Forest, down by the railroad tracks, half a mile from the
University of Michigan campus, in a house that had only a stove, a
refrigerator, and three mattresses, one for each bedroom. We slept
on the mattresses on the floor. In the morning we fled the house
and went to classes. In the evening we met in a bar called The
Ideal, a very dark place with a grim erotic mood. Until closing
time, we drank with friends. Then we walked back to the house.
Months passed. The house remained hollow. Passing freight trains
filled the empty rooms with banging iron. Our voices, magnified
by emptiness, were loud; our laughter sounded hysterical. It was a
bleak and uncomfortable way to live and, since we ate meals out,
expensive. We didn't have a coffeepot. We didn't have a cup or a
spoon. We didn't because we didn't. I don't know why. There was
no pleasure in such deprivation, or in the cold bare floors and walls.
One night at The Ideal, a bartender said he knew of an abandoned

house fifteen miles outside of town. Full of furniture. He drew us a map on a paper napkin.

"It's like salvaging goods from a sunken ship," said Norden, a shrewd light in his eyes, yellowish, small, set high in the long blade of his face. A narrow nose, pointed mouth, front teeth slightly exposed, ratlike. He nodded yes-yes-yes to Forest and me. His mathematician's mind, very quick, was reflected in his skinny, nervous body, everywhere jerky and impulsive. He'd reach for his beer glass and knock it over. He'd walk into doorjambs and the sharp edges of things. He was otherwise unlucky, too, always losing important stuff—eyeglasses, fountain pen, wallet, notebooks. His girlfriend's dog bit him on the mouth. He rode his bicycle over a sewer grate. The front wheel caught, flinging him across the handlebars into the street. He stood up with torn hands and knees, laughing. Gifted in math but a complete *shlimazel*. The more he wanted to go, the more it felt unwise, unlucky. I offered no opinion and waited for Forest.

He had a different ethos. Big-boned, blond, a wide face, sleepy gray eyes, and a slow heavy mouth. He could read five languages, and he spoke them all in a whiny Boston accent; a squeal almost, surprising in a big man. His German could pass for his Spanish. He looked up from the bartender's map, then left his bar stool and walked toward the street door, carrying himself with judicious dignity, anticipating the day when he'd be bigger and heavier and read ten languages. "I'll fetch my flashlight," he said. "Borrow the landlord's pickup, Norden. Meet us at home." He assumed we'd follow him into the street. We did.

Driving in the warm October night beneath a yellow moon, Norden at the wheel, I saw flat shining fields and scattered stands of oak and pine fly past on either side. The house was where the bartender's map said it would be, floating like a black barge in a lake of black grass, a hundred feet from the road. Two stories, bungalow-style; an external chimney and an enclosed front porch.

The moonlight was strong. No clouds. Forest didn't use his flashlight, since it could be seen miles away and the countryside was patrolled. We trudged in tall grass, stumbled into ruts. Vegetables had once been planted here. The earth was stonelike now, the grass stiff, splintery. Norden jumped onto the porch and strode to the door. "Nailed shut," he said. He began kicking it. Forest and I stepped onto the porch, forced a window up, and slid beneath the sash. Norden stopped kicking.

In palpable gloom, we stood together trying to sense the proportions of the parlor. Moonlight, cut off by the thrust of the porch roof, didn't enter the room. My skin, sensitized by darkness, took incomprehensible messages, but I knew something in front of us was large. Forest turned on his flashlight. "Nobody move."

We saw a black hole at our feet. One step plunged us. Forest traced the edge of the hole with his light and poked into the center. The beam caught an object. Smashed, spewing wires like an explosive disembowelment, keys streaming along a jumbled, twisted line—an upright piano in the bottom of the hole, obscene and tragic-looking. The floor had collapsed, dropping it through the rug, trailing hairy streamers of wool.

Forest moved the light away. Blackness gobbled piano. Forest's light then discovered a sofa, a highboy, chairs, standing lamps, framed portrait-photographs, and a door. We edged around the hole, then through the door into a kitchen with a brick floor and a high, square, five-legged farm table in the center. Four plates and mugs, with knives, forks, and spoons, had been set. A newspaper lay folded across one plate. A family was about to arrive, sit, eat breakfast. It suggested memorial statuary, pure waiting, without any expectation.

I stayed close behind Norden, he behind Forest, who led us back through the parlor and around the piano-hole to a staircase. In a second-floor bedroom stood a double bed with a tall walnut headboard, leafy design across the top. Whoever carved it had good hands; good feeling for sleep. The high dark wood invited you to lie down as if beneath a mighty tree. A quilt of silky pieces lay on the bed, lavenders, silvers, and grays. It had a religious feeling, sensuous, muted, very serious. I didn't want to touch anything, let alone take. "We'll take that dresser and go," said Norden. No enthusiasm in his voice, only anxiety to get it over with; get out.

Forest stepped to a dresser opposite the bed. "Not heavy." It was heavy. Solid maple. Lifting together, we shuffled out of the bedroom to the stairs, Norden at the front, me in the middle, my spine sliding along the banister. Halfway down, the dresser jammed. Forest, above me, took the weight on his knees. Norden pressed up from below, weight against his chest. "Lift higher," he said, "free it." The baseboard stabbed through the slickness of my palms, seeking bone. Forest, wheezing, heaved left and right. "Come on, free it." The dresser was adamant. My legs trembled. My neck swelled with heat and pressure. I wanted to kick the son-of-a-bitch. Then, with imperceptible suddenness, the dresser became weightless and the darkness closed in, embraced us softly, affectionately, as if to say, "I know you're really good boys."

I was keen as a cat. Forest whispered, "Did you hear it?"

I let go, slithering free of the dresser before it crashed. Forest hurtled downstairs on hands and knees. The back of Norden's shirt in my fist, I swerved with him at the hole. Forest was right behind me, shoving my back as I dove behind Norden through the space at the bottom of the window. We hit the porch and scrambled into the field, running. Grass lashed my legs like wires. Struggling against his bulk, Forest made speed for a big man.

In the cab of the pickup, Norden slapped his pockets. "Lost the key." Forest punched the dashboard with his thick fist, as if not to punch him. I saw the key sticking out of the ignition cylinder and said, "There." Norden's hand twisted it. His other hand flicked on the headlights. The engine lurched. The road leaped at us.

None of us knew what we'd heard in the farmhouse.

In the days that followed, we went to local junk shops and bought a couch, kitchen table, rug, and curtains. Then we had a coffeepot, cups, spoons, and food in the refrigerator. We ate breakfast at home. Cups, spoons, knives, forks; all different shapes and sizes plucked off shelves and scooped out of bins. They clattered against the porcelain of the sink and felt good being soaped. Lingering at the kitchen table on a winter morning, I listened to a freight train banging and clanking by. When it had passed, I listened to silence. No less definite. Sparrows twittered just outside the window, but I continued to hear, beyond them, a universe of silence, intolerant of intrusions before the moment assigned.

Published as "The Abandoned Farmhouse: A Memoir" in *Grand Street*, Summer 1984, and reprinted in *Shuffle* (Farrar, Straus and Giroux, 1990).

a sentimental memoir

IN THE WINTER OF 1953, I was working in a collection agency near Chambers Street in Manhattan. I'd held the job all through college while living at home with my parents. The agency pursued debtors who were in flight throughout the United States and constantly changing their names. My job was to decipher and put together information about these debtors as it arrived in the mail from other debt collectors. It seemed to me amazing that thousands of people were making money by hunting for thousands of people who owed money. We kept one-third of any debt we collected. The job wasn't extremely interesting, but it also wasn't boring. It paid well enough, and I kept my own hours. I sometimes felt sorry for the debtors, but there was a kind of intellectual and moral satisfaction in running them down. When I found some debtor, my boss took over. He would then harass the debtor, yelling on the phone or threatening him in letters, until the poor frightened man paid what he owed in part or whole. I don't remember any women debtors, but this was the old days when it was mainly men who failed in business or cheated and stole and then fled and assumed new identities. They would try to start life over in a new town, but we would find them sooner or later.

One day a literary friend told me that Professor Austin Warren of the University of Michigan, and coauthor of a famous book called *Theory of Literature*, was going to teach a night class at the Washington Square campus of NYU. The friend said Warren was really good, and not to be missed. So I left work early to attend his first class. When I arrived, I found every chair taken and a lot of students sitting on the floor. The air was dense with sweaty clothes, perfumes, tobacco gas, and nameless effusions of the city. Even the light seemed soiled. It had a dingy glare, an effect of indoor electric light in winter in Manhattan, an ether that yellowed and blurred the weary faces in the room. Many had come from offices uptown and downtown, hustling against the rush-hour pressure of masses going home to dinner and television. I supposed Warren had to be very good to draw this many students. They were all probably in a Ph.D. program. But I wasn't a graduate student. I merely loved books, and I believed that my literary interests were self-indulgent and immoral, because they were of no practical value. Warren was going to talk about Henry James, whose novels were obsessed with the exquisitata of consciousness, mainly among people who didn't work. Some characters who did, like the governess in *The Turn of the Screw* or the "publishing scoundrel" in *The Aspern Papers*, were evil. It occurred to me that I would do better to forget literature, especially Henry James, and go to medical school. Yet, anonymous among the city's anonymous innumerables, I had rushed to this squalid room excited by incoherent hope, as if there were something in it for me.

I found a place where I could lean against a window ledge. Outside, directly below, I could see the wintry trees and winding paths of Washington Square Park. It seemed bleak and dismal.

When Warren arrived, he stepped by the students on the floor and went quickly to the front, where there was no desk, only a small library table. He took off his coat and dropped it on the table. Then he faced the class and stabbed the floor with his cane. Holding up a book, he said in a strong voice, "Henry James lived here. He walked these streets in Washington Square." Warren smiled with fierce exultation. The class was under way. I was electrified.

I'd never heard a professor speak with such passion. Warren seemed to believe Henry James was "important" and that it was a great privilege for all of us to be here talking about his work. Indeed, he had graced the local streets with his important presence. Warren's voice and manner and posture and cane insisted that we believe and that we exult in the belief. It is no exaggeration when I say that, for the first time in years, I felt it was all right not to be in medical school. In a sense I felt saved.

Warren offered no introduction to his course. He didn't mention exams, and said nothing about any papers the class would write. He told us what novels we would read, then simply began reading aloud from James's novel *Washington Square*, stopping occasionally to notice the adverbs, or to say, "Comma," or "Semicolon." Stopping, he would look up at us and wait and say no more. It was baffling at first, but, in the way a child learns a language, I began to appreciate Jamesian punctuation for its delicate and minuscule refinements of tone and meaning. To appreciate is not to say I was crazy about it. I sometimes thought it was a tedious and self-regarding distraction from very good stories about sex and money. But Warren loved James and, as only a superb critic is able to do, he put me in the mood where I could hear what he heard, and feel what he felt.

Warren never mangled sentences with analysis. He called attention to metaphors and images and sometimes to just a single word. He relished meanings, not merely as meanings, but rather for how they were achieved and how they lived on the page. He urged us always to "get it," to hear the voice and savor its play of implication. It is impossible to reproduce Warren's effect since you had to be in the room with him to be struck by it. I can say only that, in Warren's class, literary pleasures and understanding were simultaneous.

The first class was essentially a reading lesson, or a kind of sermon in which he exhorted us to hear and to feel what is said in the book. Warren's approach required concentration, the sort you might associate with prayer. His sermon was consistent in spirit with the fifties, a religio-literary time dominated by the talmudic practices of the New Critics, many of whom were Christians. Some were excellent poets, and all wrote excellent prose. In those days, a critic's job of interpretation included judgment of value and could have the force of revelation. Critical essays resembled works of art. They were splendid in sensibility and densely intellectual and they inspired interest in the numinous qualities of words. Essays were so carefully written as to seem chiseled, sentence by sentence, toward the revelation of otherwise ineffable meanings. In this spirit Warren professed. I thought the New Critics were giants. I still think so.

Warren didn't use notes in his lectures, or make formal presentations. He would read aloud—which is literally to lecture—and

then ask questions that touched upon unique particulars of a
writer's style in prose or verse. The excitement I felt in his class was
always tied to the connection with the innerness of writers that he
helped me to feel. I'd had professors of English who were excellent
for other reasons, but except for a few who were poets, none who
effected Warren's kind of literary intimacy in the classroom. I
thought he was not merely brilliant and learned but also deeply
generous, and I loved him for that.

Warren was an exceedingly nervous man who wore a black suit
and vest, and stood facing the class throughout the hour. I don't
remember him ever sitting, except in seminars where all the students sat on either side of a long table. Occasionally, he wandered
about the room. He didn't smoke, though it was very common for
professors and students to light up during lectures. They dropped
cigarette butts on the yellow oak floor of classrooms, or on the dark
linoleum of the hallways. Nobody ever complained about the
scarred and messy floors or rancid air. Cigarettes, like literary religiosity, made some claim about a person's serious relation to the
era. Twenty million Russians had been killed in the Second World
War, and everyone had heard about the Nazi concentration camps.
There were college students who had fought in horrific battles in
Italy and France. The atom bomb had been dropped on urban pop-
ulations. Considering the bomb, Camus saw no reason to quit
smoking. He and other major novelists wrote sensationally about
murder. One of Sarraute's weird heroines feels her lover's actual,
not orgasmic, death flow into her body. Professional athletes
smoked, even in the locker room. You have only to look at the
placid demeanor and jolly eyes of contemporary entertainers and
professors to see that we no longer smoke.

In one hand Warren held a book open to the page he was talk-

ing about. In the other hand he held a pencil, squeezing and twisting it in his fingers. He never spoke at length but would read aloud
until he was stopped by an interesting word or phrase. He might
mark it with his pencil, slashing the page with strong black lines, and
then his dark eyes, enlarged by thick, black-framed glasses, looked
up full of light and pleasure, as if deliciously entertained by meanings. He'd ask a question. While waiting for an answer, the tension
in his hand became so strong that his pencil sometimes snapped in
two. If no answer came, he'd go on as if he'd asked no question.

Before the end of that semester, I applied to graduate school at
the University of Michigan and soon thereafter quit my job at the
collection agency. I'd been outside of New York only two or three
times and I never imagined that I might live anywhere else, in
another mental climate. My mother said, "Why would anyone
want to live outside of New York? In New York you have the theater." She meant the Yiddish theater downtown, where she had
probably been four times in the last twenty years. What she really
meant was that New York wasn't Poland. The unsaid argument was
compelling, but shortly after Warren returned to Michigan I followed him, riding a train called the Wolverine from Grand Central
Station to Ann Arbor.

It was dark night when I left the city, and early morning when
I arrived in a midwestern college town and stepped from the train
into a land of no tall buildings. I had reserved a room in a dormitory on campus. I didn't want to live alone. I was about twenty
years old, and had always lived with my parents, and almost never
eaten anything but my mother's cooking, which was strictly kosher.
I'd read books and had sexual experience, but all that happened
in Manhattan. Outside Manhattan, I'd had no experience at all. I
didn't even know how to drive. I learned, eventually, on the Penn-

sylvania Turnpike, when my school friend who owned the car became too tired to drive the rest of the way to New York. The car drifted a little when I took the wheel, but after a few minutes I got the hang of it.

In my second year in Ann Arbor, I moved out of the dormitory and into an apartment with two other graduate students. In New York most of my friends were Jews. Only one was black. In Michigan most of my friends were Christians. A dozen or so were black. Some were artists. Some were athletes who came from places like Arkansas, Texas, and Indiana. I had learned to drive, and I was eating anything. Around this time I became Warren's teaching assistant.

Warren once said that his cleaning lady called him "Reverend Warren." How pleasing and delightfully absurd, he thought. But she had good reason. His black suit gave him an air of ministerial formality. A heavy Eastern Orthodox silver cross hung from a chain about his neck and lay against the middle of his chest. The cross was hidden by his jacket, which he kept buttoned, but he sometimes let the cross swing free. He always wore a tie and a white shirt. The collar never looked quite clean. His trousers were cut so short that you could see his socks when he walked.

Warren walked confusedly, hesitantly. He might stop and abruptly change direction, as if he'd forgotten, then suddenly remembered, where he wanted to go. He walked with his cane, his posture erect and dignified, as if obliged by his calling to be correct in public. He was short, but there was a tall spirit in his posture. His face was sometimes flushed very red, sometimes blazing with boils. He held his head high, and his demeanor was proud as well as red. He always seemed alert, almost feverishly alert, and when he looked at you there was terrible expectation in his eyes, as if he were looking at a gifted child, anticipating its golden remark. His look filled me with pleasure and dread. I was glad that he thought I had something to say, but certain it would be stupid. He was generous in expectation, but if a student was hopelessly wrong in answering a question, Warren might pounce on the answer and, with hungry eagerness, say, "Yes? Yes? Please do continue." Forced to continue, the student babbled vacantly or fell into an incoherent stammer of personal darkness. I'd writhe with pity and contempt, grateful not to have drawn Warren's attention, and I would remind myself never to speak in class.

He welcomed discussion, though not for its own sake. It wasn't enough to say what you thought if you said it only because you thought it. Warren once turned to me and, to my horror, said, "Leonard, what does T. S. Eliot mean by 'April is the cruelest month'?" It should have been very easy to answer, but I became deranged and began wondering how cruel were the other months. I muttered, "He means what he says." Warren said, "Ipse dixit," and let the question go. I slumped in my chair and was so ashamed with so much blood collected in my head that I couldn't hear anything more during the hour.

Warren thought highly of T. S. Eliot, so I tried to read the verse as verse and forget his weird mystical religiosity and hatred of Jews. Much of it was unintelligible and set my teeth on edge, but I would submit to Eliot's peculiar tone and sink into a trancelike condition, waiting for the value to arrive. Occasionally, I could almost take pleasure in his lines and images. I assumed it was mainly Eliot's tone that had impressed so many good critics, but I don't know. Most of his work remained unavailable to me.

Warren wore his black suit even during the summer. On one hot afternoon, he said to a nun who was taking the class that he

and she were alike in the formality of their clothing and their dedication to a calling. She didn't disagree, but simply lowered her
head. I have no idea what she thought. The sober drama of Warren's suit contrasted with his red, boil-infested face, an effect of too
much bourbon and an obscure psychological anguish. His face
could seem frightening and pathetic, but he exuded warmth and he
had spontaneous, unaffected, good humor. He also had a dark,
powerful laugh, surprising in a man his size. He might look like
hell, but I'd seen him look depressed only once, late at night, when
he phoned to ask me to bring him a bottle of Jim Beam bourbon.

Warren occasionally appeared in class slightly disheveled, a
shirttail trailing below his vest, his fly not completely zipped. I
was too conscious of his appearance, too much aware of the red
face and the boils and the least disarray of his clothing ever to feel
perfectly comfortable, not even when he was being funny and making the students laugh, which was fairly often. He wasn't an entertainer, however, or a type of ingratiating professor. From the
moment he entered the room he was immensely present, sensational in his colors and dignified in posture, and he spoke with precision and terseness much the way he wrote critical prose. He
referred to himself as "your venerable mentor." His manner was
Nabokovian in its mix of erudition, irony, steely intelligence, wit,
and an occasional touch of childlike silliness.

One Saturday afternoon, some students took Warren to a football game. They wanted to give him something of their experience
and pleasure. I imagined Warren with black suit and cane, walking
among the thousands who streamed along routes through Ann
Arbor on Saturday's weekly fall pilgrimage to the holy stadium.
The town would become desolate and still during games. Now and

then, from half a mile away, you would hear the dim oceanic roar of a hundred thousand cheering. When I stayed home on Saturday afternoon, the cheering made me feel isolated and unnatural. Some friends liked to go to the games and smoke marijuana. They could float amid the rage while gazing on the action far below. After the game Warren attended, he had no idea which team had won, but said that he'd relished the patterns and compared it to ballet.

Like the students who took Warren to the football game, I wanted to give him something of the popular culture that mattered to me, so I brought him jazz records, Charlie Parker, MJQ, Cal Tjader, Dizzy Gillespie. Warren listened and, finally, straining for a positive response, said Cal Tjader's vibraphone put him in mind of a Christmas tree. He seemed indifferent to Mongo Santamaria on bongos or Dizzy's horn. I didn't bring him any more jazz after that.

My response to Warren was excessively emotional, I suppose, but I greatly admired other professors, too; for example, Susanne K. Langer, whose lectures were careful, logical, and beautifully formed. She didn't ask you to "get it," but gave to the class what she'd already quite thoroughly gotten. She was in her late sixties, I think, and rather frail. One of her eyelids would fall as she spoke. She kept pushing it back up. She lectured straight through the hour. Her lectures were like her prose, every word chosen for exact sense and perfect clarity. Her delivery was plain, steady, undramatic, and lucid. She seemed a pure medium of mind, interposing no personality, no politics, and no desire for transcendence between the material and the students. I was nuts about her, too, though very differently from Warren.

I don't think I ever said a word to Warren that didn't sound to my ears deeply stupid, and I never left his office without feeling I'd somehow shamed myself. I spent a good deal of time with him, and he was always friendly, but I didn't think of myself as his friend. I knew him only in external ways: his appearance and manner and what I took from his critical essays. I was in awe of the spectacle he made of waiflike, high-strung, disheveled, ministerial nobility.

Many others adored Warren as much as I did, and, regardless of his warmth and humor, were intimidated by him. My best friend at the time, Julian Boyd, once visited Warren's office, and when Warren said, "Please sit down," Julian snatched off his glasses, placed them on the seat of his chair, and sat on them.

Another graduate student was invited to dinner at Warren's apartment. When he arrived, Warren said, "Let me take your coat," and stepped behind him. The student felt Warren lift the coat from his shoulders. Warren hovered behind the student in the small foyer, and then hangers rattled in the closet. The student waited, not daring to look behind him, hardly breathing, and then he felt his coat being replaced on his shoulders. Warren said, "It was so good of you to come to dinner." The student said good night and went home.

To a self-destructive excess, in my adoration of Warren, I drank Jim Beam, his favorite brand of bourbon. I also tried to read any book he mentioned, as well as his books, essays, and reviews. I could have repeated his ideas about Crashaw, Pope, Kafka, Stevens, and others, but what I now remember best is that I read the way he did, with a pencil in hand, marking the pages with his kind of impassioned underlining. I, too, slashed at words and sentences, and scrawled "Yes!" in the margins exactly as Warren did when he agreed with a passage. I made such scribbles in the hope of spiritual ascendancy, but it was only imitative and mechanical. I would read and slash with great enthusiasm and hope for the value to register. Sometimes it didn't.

Warren once gave me a book and wrote across the title page, "To Leonard, My son in Christ." He considered me an honorary Christian. The question of personal identity was more difficult in those days than now, since it was indeed personal, not political. I knew that Warren's son in Christ I wasn't.

When I became Warren's teaching assistant, people in the English department said that he might phone me late at night and ask me to buy a bottle of Jim Beam and bring it to his Church Street apartment, and that Warren might appear at the door wearing the robes of a priest, a heavy cross, and the skullcap of an Orthodox Jew. I was told that his apartment was lighted by candles and reeked of incense. I was told that I would see heavy Boston furniture and an altar in the living room and a harmonium against the wall. Much about Warren was known. Little was left for me to discover, but I looked forward to seeing for myself.

One afternoon, as I sat in Warren's apartment reading and grading his students' papers, there was a thunderous blast of chords from the harmonium five feet away, against the wall behind me. I whirled about and saw Warren pounding the instrument. He called to me above the booming voluminous tones and nasal whining of the instrument, "Do you know this music, Leonard?"

I said, "No."

He said, "You don't think it's 'Yankee Doodle,' do you?"

I said, "No."

He called out again, still pounding, "It was written by Luther. Now do you know it?"

"No," I said. I didn't believe Luther would know it, either.

As Warren's teaching assistant, I read most, and sometimes all, of his students' papers. I wrote comments on them and gave them a grade. Even if my comments indicated the student was brain-dead, the grade was likely to be an A because Warren always gave students an A. When I finished reading the papers, Warren glanced at my comments and the grades, and he would say, "Very judicious, Leonard." He pronounced my name "Linurd."

In Warren's class there was a girl who I tried not to look at. I gave her papers to Warren for comments and a grade. I wanted no opinion of her mind. I didn't want her to come up to me after class to discuss her work. There was nothing I wanted more than to stand close to her and talk to her, but it seemed too frightening as well as incorrect. After class, I'd go away weirdly exhilarated, as if there were an exciting connection between us, though I never spoke to her. My job as Austin Warren's teaching assistant forbade the least suggestion of hanky-panky with one of his students. Being insanely in love made no difference.

The girl had a slender boyish figure and blondish hair. I thought nobody but me considered her striking or had noticed the subtle perfection of her beautiful face. When I told my friend Julian that the most beautiful girl in Michigan was in Warren's class, he named her. He told me that she modeled naked for art students, she had a horrible reputation for licentiousness, everybody knew who she was, and that he was in love with her, too. I decided that I was ready to forgive her everything. To forgive a girl was a very popular sentiment of the day. There were plays, novels, and movies about forgiving bad girls. As for the girl I was ready to forgive, I now suppose there were a couple of hundred other men who were forgiving her at the same time, all of us subject to a sort of spiritual narcissism that has long since gone out of the world. Too bad, I think, since it had extraordinary intensity and made a man feel tortured by goodness, which is a very high order of feeling.

It was my job to attend Warren's class. I waited outside Haven Hall, the building where his class was held, and watched for him to appear at the far end of the quadrangle. When he arrived, he would pause and look about, a small, still, black-suited man with a cane amid the hurrying crowd of students. If he headed toward the wrong building, I would approach and wait at the margin of his vision. When he noticed me, I would walk beside him as if nothing were amiss, chatting about trivial business as I edged him toward Haven Hall.

The walk from his apartment to campus was only a few blocks, but the Ann Arbor streets, with their huge trees, and the energy of thousands of students, and the savagery of cars and trucks, became increasingly difficult for Warren. He arrived later and later at class meetings. Half the students waited. The other half, one by one, got up and left. I'd feel embarrassed for Warren and angry, but even when forty minutes late he never came to an empty room.

After the final grades for Warren's class had been turned in, I decided to phone the girl. Barely able to breathe, I said my name and told her I was Warren's assistant. She laughed with affectionate and pitying good humor and said, "What took you so long?"

She sounded healthy and clear in feelings, very different from me. I was doubtful and murky, and in awe of her power. But she had laughed. It was intimate and encouraging laughter. The next night I went to her dormitory, a long, low brick building in the Gothic style, with girls swarming in its bowels. No men ventured beyond the dormitory desk. In those days, there were men and girls.

I waited at the desk until the girl appeared. I asked if she'd like to go to dinner or a movie. "Let's go to your place," she said, and took my arm as if we knew each other well and were easy and natural together. I remember nothing of the walk from the dormitory. An hour later we were in bed. We made love without first smoking marijuana or listening to my collection of Chet Baker records. I had no virginity to lose, but when sex happened with guiltless and astonishing speed, I lost my innocence. This happened in the Midwest, not Manhattan.

In a romantic delirium, I said, "Let's go away."

"Where?"

"Someplace nobody knows us."

She answered in a sweetly ironic tone, "I'd go to Detroit with you."

My room was bleak: a beat-up pine dresser, and a mattress on the floor, stacks of books and a metal ashtray. No pictures. The bleakness made the love feeling real in the way of noir movies. The grim passion of restricted rooms. She probably recognized the symptoms of morbidity and knew how I felt, since men were always falling in love with her. She was affectionate and accommodating. She wasn't coy, or coquettish, or seductive. She was plain, straightforward, high-spirited, and faithless. There would always be other men. Her thing was otherness.

Around midnight my roommate knocked at the door and whispered, "Professor Warren," then opened the door a little and handed the phone to me. Warren wanted a bottle of Jim Beam. I didn't wonder about what I had to do. She didn't, either. We dressed. Maybe I kissed her good night. I don't remember. I left her in the apartment chatting with my roommate, borrowed his bicycle, rode to a liquor store, and then sped to Warren's place.

I knocked and waited long minutes. When the door opened, I smelled incense and saw candlelight shivering on the pine paneling of the apartment walls. Warren was in his priestly attire, his face red and swollen, his voice ragged, heavily slurred. I handed him the bottle, which he took without meeting my eye and said, "Thank you, Linurd."

I'd gone from bed to temple, trailing sexual odors. Churning the pedals, bent low over the handlebars, I went flying home through empty silent streets where huge trees arched over me, cathedral-like, in a high, solemn, grieving curve. The girl would be gone when I returned and I would be miserable.

We saw each other a few more times, and I met her parents once when they visited the campus. Her mother was a beautiful woman with eyes that seemed to grieve for you even before you fall in love with her and are lost. She was slightly taller than her husband, a colorless man with the genial, suffering expression of a friendly drunk.

I soon lost the girl to a man who lost her to another. She left a trail of disjecta membra from west to east and back. Her fatal type ceased to exist during the sixties, when promiscuity became not only common but commonly confessed. I thought she was unique until I read Mary McCarthy's "intellectual autobiography." She says nice girls like herself slept with countless men, sometimes two or three a day, and just didn't talk about it.

The last time I saw Warren, he'd had a nervous collapse and was in a hospital bed. Even lying on his back, head and shoulders propped up by pillows, he was a sensational presence and he seemed happy, rather as if his collapse were an achievement. A dozen books were stacked on the table beside his bed. I noticed the

Sherlock Holmes detective stories. I'd never learned much about Warren's past. People talked about him constantly, but it was usually anecdotal, caricaturing rather than illuminating. Nobody seemed to know what caused his suffering. He'd been married and his wife had died young, but that was long ago.

I dropped out of graduate school in the summer of 1956, around the time of his collapse, and returned to New York with a case of "nonspecific urethritis," a form of venereal disease I'd contracted from the girl, I suppose, because there had been nobody else. A few years later I returned to graduate school at Berkeley rather than Ann Arbor. Sometime in 1960, I was browsing in Moe's, then a musty, shadowy secondhand bookstore on Telegraph Avenue, and I picked up an old edition of *Washington Square*. Page after page had been heavily scored by black underlining, and the margins were scrawled with exclamations of approval, "Yes!" "Indeed!" All in Warren's handwriting. I was surprised and deeply moved, then suspicious, then shaken. The markings were too extravagantly Warren's. It wasn't his distinctive energy but a mockery of it. Looking through the book, I discovered that it had been manufactured with a section of pages upside down, and many pages were missing. It was unreadable. Someone had attacked the book with an imitation of Warren's manner.

I remembered the shame I'd sometimes felt in his company, and I felt it again. I'd done nothing shameful, but feelings have a life of their own and they accused me. Of what, I don't know. I'd adored Warren. Maybe adoration has a dark side, and mine had been too much repressed. Maybe it was just that times had changed and the latest cultural radiations were streaming into my soul. Everything Warren represented was antithetical to the mood of the new and rebellious masses, not that he had ever been with it. I thought of

Warren in his ministerial black suit stopped amid the hurrying crowds of students. How still and small he looked. He held himself imperiously erect, his head high, glancing here and there, as though searching for something that would tell him where he was, or why he stood in this place.

A version of this memoir was published as "Professor Warren's Disciple" in *The New York Times Magazine*, May 12, 1996.

a berkeley memoir

SOON AFTER I CAME TO BERKELEY to begin graduate work in English, I got into a fight with a married couple in my apartment on Le Roy Avenue.

I knew about them through friends. Barry Glock had a degree in geology, but wanted to be a sculptor. His wife, Marla, was a painter. We all came from New York. Marla and I were alumni of the same high school, Music and Art, but we hadn't met until just before the fight. City, school, friends—we had much in common.

Nevertheless, Barry trapped my head in a stranglehold and Marla dragged her fingernails down my face. The fight was about money.

Barry and I locked together, twisting, stumbling. Marla leaped after my rigidified head, slashing at it. Her cries and curses awakened my roommate. He bounded into the living room in his pajamas. Tall, crew-cut, blond kid from San Diego. Engineering student, he went to classes with a slide rule dangling from his belt. Mechanical pencils sprouted from his shirt pocket like asparagus tips. He'd never before witnessed critical intercourse among East Coast intelligentsia. His name was Ted Gidding.

Instead of studying the scene—thus enlarging his soul—Ted phoned the cops. They arrived quickly. The fight was over. My face carried a spray of bleeding rips, the record of Marla's fingernails. I could have put her out of action by kicking her, but this was 1958. I was sentimental and sexist.

The cops were young men. Marla, small and pretty, made herself smaller. She did it with her voice, simpering how I owed her and Barry thirty-five dollars, their cleaning deposit on the apartment. I protested, shouting through the red rags of my face: "The landlord said don't give them money. The landlord—not I—must return their deposit. But only after they fix the holes they made in every wall while living here before me."

The cops said to take our disagreement to court. If we fought any more they'd feel obliged to arrest us. They spoke in the polite manner for which Berkeley cops were famous. Marla's fingernails were mooned in my blood. Her eyes were hot and exquisite. "Come, let's go," she said. Barry and the cops followed her out. Two days after the fight, she and Barry returned, spackled the holes. The landlord gave them thirty-five dollars. It could have been that simple. But she needed the fight, and months later, telling our friends what she'd done to me, she said, "It feels good to mutilate the face of a fairy."

That they wanted to steal my money—fellow New Yorker and Music-and-Arter, not to mention Jew—was depressing. More depressing, they wanted to kill me because I wouldn't let them steal it. When the cops were gone, I didn't forget the incident and go to sleep. Psycho-moral problems demanded analysis. Ted looked uncomfortable standing barefoot in pajamas. It wasn't easy to ignore the horrible condition of my face.

"Tell me if I'm wrong. Barry, influenced by his wife, abandoned geology to be a sculptor, an artist. Like her. But Barry Glock isn't Michelangelo. He looks at a rock, he sees the history of the earth, not the future of forms. In his heart he knows he must fail, make himself miserable. Rocks once made him happy. See? A bitter man, he gets into fights. When Barry is a total wretch, she'll divorce him. He'll pay alimony the rest of his life while he chisels his rocks."

Ted, rubbing his eyes, slumped and sighed. No words. No personal interpretation. Perhaps he considered Barry, Marla, and me bad people. Even so I wanted him to say a word. It might bear the odor of anti-Semitism. For a mean reason, I wanted to smell it. At last he said, "There was a question of money. I have to sleep. Early tomorrow I'm going sailing. Like to come?"

"No."

The invitation seemed insensitive. To me, a great body of water like San Francisco Bay was for sewage. Sailing was for tugboats. Ted said good night and went to sleep. I said good night and stayed up, analyzing the motives of people who go sailing.

NEXT MORNING a telegram came from Ian Watt of the Berkeley English department. It said show up for an interview at one o'clock if I wanted to be considered for a job as a teaching assistant. I had no other income; I needed the job. First I needed a shave. About to shave, I saw my face. It looked like a voodoo mask. I remembered Marla's hooks tearing at my eyes and I had a vision: New York was tearing at my eyes. Why? Because I didn't want to live there anymore. I wanted to live in Berkeley, where roses and blackberries grow in the streets, where light is Parisian, where Ted Gidding sleeps ten hours a night, doesn't like talk, and goes sailing year-round; where the hills are luscious with live oaks and beautiful houses; where famous scholars, who refused jobs in the East, dash gaily from the library to cocktail parties chattering about Guggenheim Fellowships and ACLS awards; where on a hilltop commanding city and bay a legendary laboratory stands, defended by a Cyclone fence and armed guards. Its lights burn ceaselessly. Icy brain. Inside, a throng of Nobel laureates make bombs, whistle melodies from Beethoven's string quartets, and reminisce about undergraduate days at Heidelberg. It was a Berkeley morning, sweet, shining with love. I wanted to be of this place, this beauty, power, and happiness, but my face, my face . . .

In black sunglasses and a dark suit I arrived for the interview. I looked like a pimp from Vegas. Before Watt could appreciate me, I said, "I had a fight last night. This face doesn't count."

During the Second World War, Watt spent time in a Japanese concentration camp. He'd seen worse faces. More pertinent is that he was handsome, broad shouldered, tastefully dressed. Looking at him through black glasses, I had an impression of myself: ugly, creepy, frightened. Watt nodded, then asked, "With whom did you study before coming to Berkeley?" I named professors at NYU and the University of Michigan. His expression became cheerful and encouraging, yet faintly poisoned by pity. I knew I hadn't gotten the job. In fact I had. It paid for my rent and food during the next two years while I attended classes in English and philosophy.

Thus, my introduction to Berkeley was grotesque and ironical. Had there been no fight my face would have been normal. I might not have gotten the job. If Watt hadn't suffered in a concentration camp, he might have given the job to another candidate, a cleaner type. All in all, because the Japanese bombed Pearl Harbor, I, who at the lucky moment was mutilated by a nasty bitch from the Bronx while her half-wit husband strangled me, got the job.

I remember a philosophy seminar conducted by J. L. Austin and a seminar in English conducted by J. McNulty. In a vague way these professors looked alike, versions of the genetic genius that produced Fred Astaire. Bony, sharp, pale. A tension in their bodies at once brittle and languid. They seemed figures of needle precision. Austin also had tremendous intelligence. His prose, like the dancing of Astaire, is beautiful and made of steel. McNulty had the precision. He edited Harington's translation of *Orlando Furioso*. A day never passes when somebody doesn't point to this fat book and say it contains not a single spelling error. From these similar, extremely different professors, I gathered something exceedingly general about the University of California at Berkeley. It accommodates extremes. This was true in the fifties. It is still true.

During the sixties, some faculty stars accepted jobs in the East. But some have gratefully returned. The library isn't as good as it used to be. Football and fraternities are big again along with old styles of racism and drunken bonhomie. I've been told that, at four in the morning, you can hear fraternity men singing to the sorority house next door: "Oh, I'm happy to be a Beta / And I want to fuck a Theta." However, not everything about the university gives itself to the idiocy of fashion. The beloved campus dogs, for example, still wander where they like, even into lecture halls; as awesome learning fills the air, they belch, fart, and fornicate. The new governor of the state, in whom many saw hope because he studied classics at Berkeley, turns out not to be a friend. Therefore, like San Francisco Bay, hope shrinks a little year by year. But the demands of instinct, represented not only by dogs and fraternities, continue

huge and undefeated. Though the air is murky with industrial tox-
ins, more people go jogging every day. You see bicyclists churning
up the steepest hills and, despite university rules, you see them
speeding across campus. My eight-year-old son, walking with me
to my office, was hit by a bicycle doing about forty miles per hour.
Fortunately, the cyclist was flung over the handlebars and badly
hurt. There is endless talk about the body—how to feel it deeply,
feed it naturally, heal it impeccably, transcend it completely—and
much talk about murder and rape. Population density in the Bay
Area compares now to Calcutta's, and Berkeley's Telegraph Avenue,
once very pleasant, is like the Hoogli's pestilential flux. Citizens
tend more and more to vote for conservative politicians, but there
are mansions in the hills—with luxurious cars and glorious gar-
dens—that are bastions of invincible revolutionary sentiment. A
friend's daughter, packing to leave for Barnard, included among fifteen lovely leather suitcases a twenty-four-inch color TV and her
giant-poster collection of Mao, Ho, Castro, Trotsky, Stalin, and the
Rolling Stones. When I asked if she sometimes wondered about
spiritual inconsistencies, her father answered, "Why don't you go
back to your pit in New York?"

Her father, a professor of sociology, is one of my oldest friends.
Though he makes me feel stupid, I love him. He helps me understand this place. Luxury isn't a twenty-four-inch TV set. Luxury is
always, finally, mental. Here, in Berkeley, as in exotic cooking,
irreconcilables are sublimed into deliciousness. Out my window I
see, after two years of drought, hills densely, ponderously green. My
lemon tree bulges yellow buboes. Thus, the very earth—liable any
moment to spill into the Pacific with beautiful houses and posters
of Mao—renders a complex meaning. Of course Austin and
McNulty taught here at the same time. This is Witty Land. In

every lush corner the flower of genius springs among weeds of schmuck. Red, hideous rips rayed out from my sunglasses to my hairline and jaw, but Ian Watt gave me the job. This could not have happened at Ohio State.

In Austin's seminar I never took notes lest I miss a phrase or fail to savor his least inflection. He talked once about the difference between saying you did something "inadvertently" and saying you did it "by accident." It's been long since I heard this marvelous talk, which exists now in essay form. I could check to see precisely what he meant, but I'm more interested in memory than in truth. I think he intended some connection with life, though he held us with dazzling discriminations that belong only to words. Still, I suspected he was saying something about life, where actions have consequences that are often irreversible and beyond qualification. To illuminate his discriminations between "inadvertently" and "by accident," he said to consider the example of a man who goes to shoot his donkey but shoots his neighbor's instead.

I saw the dead donkey and the frowning philosopher, shotgun smoking in his hands as he wonders whether he murdered the donkey "inadvertently" or "by accident." What follows? Something about very subtle, distinctly different ideas entailed by the use of apparently similar words. This seemed immensely interesting; it seemed to me just as interesting that beyond our institutionalized commitment to words is no less than many more words. A friend who had a degree in philosophy from Oxford, hearing me rave about this talk, said, "Do you know there is something at Oxford called Logic Lane? And do you know what a lane is? It is a path that doesn't *necessarily* go anywhere." Austin, who came from Oxford, then seemed to be saying that, in addition to our lovely luminous weather and beautiful campus, we needed a Logic Lane, and that even existentially opaque seriousness, like dead donkeys, can provide the keenest glee of mind. He was saying, perhaps inadvertently, Witty Land isn't witty enough.

BEFORE AUSTIN RETURNED TO OXFORD, where he planned to pack his things and return to Berkeley, he lectured to a large audience on the history of English words. He said words stay in the language insofar as they mean something approximately like other words that sound approximately the same. (Examples might be "snot," "snicker," "snoop.") On the other hand, words that mean very different things, but sound the same, compete radically. Their fate is variously to vanish. As always he was brilliant, and this time also passionate, strongly reiterating his theme, waving his arm as he spoke, apparently a little drunk. From where I sat behind his desk—the room was too crowded for everyone to sit in front of him—I could see that he'd slipped partly from his chair and was lecturing on one knee as he made this obliquely personal, very powerful case for himself—the word "Austin" soon to vanish from Oxford—or was it for the naturalness and inevitability of conventional order, the way things are anyhow always? I don't know what he was saying. This is what I remember guessing. A thousand years from now, as scholars search for biographical information about Austin, they may be grateful for trivia such as this.

Compared to Austin's seminar, McNulty's was the dead donkey. He never said anything interesting, though his look always suggested, beneath his smooth pale face, that knowledge lay packed into bone as neatly and tightly as his teeth. If any of us imagined we had something interesting to say, he crushed such presumption. A paper I wrote for him, full of graduate student enthusiasm, was returned with the comment that my misuse of the optative mood was evidence of moral decay. This hurt my feelings, but to be fair I confess he was right. In his seminar, I suffered moral decay. I'd tell myself McNulty is a lonely man, very sad, perhaps afraid of his students and colleagues, afraid they won't love him. But it was no use. He seemed to me stiff, dull, hateful. We were studying *The Faerie Queene*. I once liked the poem, but McNulty required that we learn to worship its sublimities by doing an ideal edition of several cantos. To impress us with the moral value of this excruciating requirement, he sneered a lot. We made mistakes. The chief mistake, week after week, was that we continued merely to be. His own being was justified by the beauty of his person. In some lights his head became a structure of antithetical knives, like a vorticist painting, and yet he walked the halls of the English department with an air of lyrical possession, as if he lived discreetly and sweetly in a wiggly secret twig pinched between his buttocks. He was overheard once saying to a colleague, "I have the gift of chastity." Austin and McNulty are now dead. Austin had cancer. McNulty, I suppose, had chastity.

In 1967 I began teaching at Berkeley and soon became less romantic about the place and able to see that the university, in its exceedingly complex character, is at once a formidable and fragile thing, and its mysteriously political essence is as far beyond my powers of understanding as are my colleagues. When I asked them for permission to tell some anecdote they told me, which might give realistic substance to this account, they said no. I promised to disguise the situations and people. They said no. I promised I wouldn't talk about the particulars of any sexual nexus between faculty and students, though it was an ancient topic, thoroughly described by Plato and known to the whole world. They said no. I swore I wouldn't ever repeat a word said at a tenure meeting where the fate of junior colleagues is determined after hours of life-embittering debate, and I would say only that you go home afterward unable to eat or sleep or remember who the hell you are, you who spoke so long and sanctimoniously about somebody's scholarship or teaching record in the deliberations of that grim convention and—though it meant the scholar might soon have to begin thinking about life in Kansas City or Detroit—you never for a moment risked your own shingled nook in the Berkeley hills with its bay view and patio bright with fuschias and camellias and plum trees and all dazzled by hummingbirds, you, whoever you are, that one who schlepped down the halls, the long halls of the department, to a colleague's office the day after you publicly, furiously repudiated his judgment and you tell him, trembling, insanely confused, you've come to take back not one word but to say you want his friendship anyhow. You put out your hand. He takes it and smiles. You feel this is impossible. You've annihilated yourself. It must be time to get out, there must be another way to live. I said, "Look, I can't talk about the university without being personal. I'll talk about myself. Let me talk about you—in disguise." They said no.

This essay was originally published in the *New Republic*, October 22, 1977.

kishkas

A NATION OF IMMIGRANTS, we adore worldly success because it proves we exist despite attenuated roots or none. But more interesting than success is its dark brother, failure, and the strange fascination with failure that haunts American literature from the apocalyptic grandeur of *Moby Dick* through the pathos of *Sister Carrie* and *Seize the Day*, or the grueling agonies of *Death of a Salesman*, or the poignant ironies of *The Great Gatsby*, *The Sun Also Rises*, *Lolita*, and innumerable short stories and poems. Imagine then millions of failed pages on failure, laboriously wrought, deeply sincere, discoloring in drawers and boxes about the land. Something very like this—unheard, unseen, immanent—is made vast and looming in "The Yachts," a frightening poem by William Carlos Williams, where he discovers a spectral thrill in the heart of failure. Williams sees the nervous and exhilarating beauty of racing yachts, and abruptly suffers an access of vision:

> . . . *a sea of faces about them in agony, in despair*

162

. . . the horror of the race dawns staggering the mind;
the whole sea . . . an entanglement of watery bodies . . .

beaten, desolate, reaching up from the dead . . .
they cry out, failing, failing!

My entanglement with watery bodies occurred mainly in Hollywood, but it began in New York, in 1979, when an editor at *Cosmopolitan* invited me to write for the magazine. I submitted a story called "The Men's Club." It was refused. Ultimately, *Esquire* published the story, and, some time later, I made it into the first chapter of a novel that was received with praise and sneering, in 1981, and went into several foreign languages even as the desolate hand reached for me.

Some reviewers said the novel is an allegory; others thought it satirizes the women's movement; one reviewer called me a "misogynist"; another said "feminist." It was as if I'd been talking to someone on the platform of a train station when a locomotive—the Zeitgeist Cannonball—rumbled by and sucked my sense after it. I felt emptied; dispossessed.

Writing the novel was easy. I liked the characters and laughed at them. These men didn't understand women, didn't even understand what they didn't understand. The subject, male friendship, wasn't new to me. Now I remembered my mother saying, when I was a kid, "You're laughing. Soon you'll be crying." She meant there was much to fear in this world. Hitler, dogs, large bodies of water, strangers. Laughter could catch the hate of an evil ear.

The phone rang with New York theater people and Hollywood. It sounded like success. I probably should have relished it, but I left town, and, for about ten days, drove alone across the country in a mood of nauseating delirium. Dogwood was in bloom from Baltimore to Birmingham, airy white rivers along the highway that simplified me, made me feel happy sometimes for fifty miles. I talked to nobody until I met a couple in a motel bar near El Paso. They owned a local ranch.

The woman said, "Bud, we are so right-wing, we're almost fascist. Do you have a gun in your car?"

"Me? No."

"No? You're driving across Texas *without a gun?*"

I wondered if I were breaking some law. The man pressed toward me. "What Luella wants to say is that we can tell you're on the left politically. I used to live in New York, too, and I know you can't help it. I know what you feel. Everything in the world ought to be divvied up. It would be the best thing. But communism won't work because most people are no damned good."

To prove his point he showed me a nine-millimeter handgun, let me heft it, feel its cold hard cogency. If one could write like that . . .

By the time I got home to Berkeley, Twentieth Century-Fox had completed negotiations with my agent for an option on the novel. The producer, Howard Gottfried, flew out to meet me. We took a walk, discussed the novel.

"I'd like to ask a question," he said.

"Okay."

"What does it mean?"

"It's about men. How some of them are."

"Sure, but what does it mean?"

I could hear them cry out, failing, failing!

What does it mean to say what it means? I only describe. Seven men in Berkeley gather to form a club . . .

A screenwriter was hired. With amazing speed, he wrote some opening scenes, but Howard didn't think they would do. They lacked a quality he was after. I wasn't permitted to read the scenes for fear of legal complications later. Howard approached other screenwriters, but all were busy writing movies. I asked him to let me try a few sketchy pages. "For free." Howard liked them. I was hired. My agent, very shocked, said, "You gave him pages?"

The word seemed exceedingly literal. What else could I give him? When I mentioned it to Howard, he said, "It isn't always called 'pages.' It's sometimes called 'shit.' A studio executive says, 'The writer turned in some shit.' "

The writer—me—believed Hollywood paid well for "shit" and the work entailed no personal sacrifice, it was pure play, innocent and lucrative happiness. It would be good for his soul to join the humble community of screenwriters. He didn't believe their stories of anguish and humiliation since they were attached to nothing a screenwriter could control and for which he could feel responsible.

Lawyers and agents created a contract. I'd turn in a first draft of a screenplay in twelve weeks. Six or seven months later, when much of the novel had been thrown out, and the intimacy and density of the male landscape was dissipated, "opened out" for the sake of a movie, Howard said, "This is it. I feel it in my kishkas, a great movie."

Once, when I had lost faith in the new material—broke down, couldn't continue—I flew to New York to talk to Howard. He was receptive, enormously encouraging, confident of the screenplay.

My feelings for it were increasingly vicarious. The creature of my contract, a writer for hire, I was always asking, "What do you think?" A surge of relief rose in me when Howard was pleased. By the end of the meeting in New York, I was high, full of ideas, anxious to get back to work. Be pleasing. "See," said Howard, "when you walked in that door, you had nothing."

It was embarrassing, but writers better than I had done this, exactly for money and the satisfaction of another person. I assumed that is how movies are written. Until then writing had been lonely, occasionally joyous but mainly miserable, with no financial reward for months and months. Now it was a social activity, a thousand phone calls and meetings, incessant talk. I'd read fresh pages over the telephone. Not one word was let stand without immediate evaluation. I felt sometimes like a secretary of the occult. When my ideas and dialogue were pleasing, it was because they struck an uncanny chord, in Howard, of rightness.

The work itself, hours and hours of typing and retyping, was torture but always relieved by flights to New York and L.A., fine hotels and restaurants, and kicks with Howard. Once, in a hotel lobby, waiting for him, I spotted a university colleague. His limp, his cane, his silvery head with black framed glasses, the lenses turning to me, perhaps seeing but not yet recognizing me before I slipped behind a pillar. I'd known him for years. I liked him, but didn't want to say hello. The hotel was too classy, not my style, not me, I wasn't here. When Howard appeared I darted to his side, then out to the street. We were off to a great dinner, rattling together about the movie. I lived in two worlds, the university and this one of cryptic pleasures.

He knew the movie business, its intricacies of money, power, and talent. He'd worked with the greats, had had success. I didn't learn much about the business, except that it really is a business, but I learned about myself, discovering a weird susceptibility to self-violation and the curiosity it inspired, watching myself as in a penitential exercise, perversely moral, without a god. It was impossible to write one line without caring, and yet everything was compromised, even the caring. The soul has ways of sliding through compromise, continuing to care, like discovering your kid is hooked on drugs when he swears he isn't—repelled, infuriated, refusing ever again to care, you care. Louis B. Mayer puts it differently: "A screenwriter is a schmuck with an Underwood." I used an Olivetti, small gray machine, nice touch.

After years in the business, a screenwriter might come to feel, always and only, "If they like my work, I like it." Liking their liking as one is turned on during sexual intercourse by the partner's moans. The phenomenon is represented in the hysteria of movie reviewers: "Wow!" "The best!" They remind you that a movie is registered in the kishkas, a physical occasion.

Lights go down and fantastic sensations of goodness begin. When the movie ends, it's also physical. Like being ripped untimely from the womb, you're disoriented, adrift, homeless, and burdened by regret, as if something could have been other than it is for you. A small, unacknowledged misery of modern times. You see it in the emerging faces, lashed by the electrical marquee, unready to go, get out, give up their dreams to others. Some remain forever in love with Tuesday Weld or Cary Grant. For others it doesn't matter what movie they've just seen. Compared to feeling real, a movie is really feeling.

Tell somebody who loves a movie that you didn't like it. See the shock and hatred in his face. "Hey, man," you say, "it's only a movie." For an instant, he could have killed you. How odd that

people can be so taken, yet even those most deeply steeped in
movies hardly ever quote lines exactly or remember accurately
what happens in a single scene, unless they've watched a movie
twice, determined really to know it. The most powerful art form of
our day depends on passionate incoherence, in our memory, for its
effects.

The eye is glazed. The mouth hangs in a slack, flat face. They
trudge, zombies of postmovie *tristesse*, back into the world. It isn't
fair. A movie is big, a human head is small.

One night, during a trip to L.A., we went to the Polo Lounge
and sat with an acquaintance of Howard who owned "a hundred
screens," or movie theaters. As we talked, a young woman came to
our table and pressed her thighs against the edge, fusing herself to it
as she stared at us. A minute passed without a word. Faintly exas-
perated, as if we should have guessed what she wanted, she said,
"My girlfriend Samantha Turetzky is late."

"Want to join us while you're waiting?" I asked. The way she
pressed the table (daddy's leg?) was original.

"I thought you'd never ask," she said, then sat with us and was
soon chatting happily. When Samantha arrived, neither said hello
to the other. Samantha took the seat beside me and began talking
mechanically, as though she'd been doing it all evening and become
oblivious to her company. She was very thin and pale, with long,
luxurious, black, romantic hair. She called herself a "working girl."
I was moved; reminded of myself, maybe. She took a brush out of
her purse and, in the middle of the Polo Lounge, began brushing
her long hair.

"I'd never do this in public," she said, and then, "I'm boring.
I'm so boring. I never even finished high school."

She talked like that, apparently, to rid herself of anxiety. Her heart wasn't in her work. I'd met others who were semiprofessionals—straight jobs on the side—whoring only for clothes, a rent-free condominium, cocaine, a man, or just attention. Samantha brushed her hair, talking every minute, and didn't seem the least calculating of her effects.

Howard's acquaintance encouraged the working girls to order dinner, then signaled a waiter and told him to put everything on his bill. A very sweet man, I thought, since two dinners at the Polo Lounge probably cost more than they could ask for their bodies; and then, as they were eating, he said good night. It seemed like a little lesson in humanity. Howard and I said good night to them a few moments later. It was easier than I expected to leave. I liked Samantha and put some of her remarks into the screenplay. I did the same later with an argument between Howard and me. I'd written "woman" at one place in the stage directions. Howard said, "But she's a whore. Write 'whore.' "

"She's a woman."

"Whore."

"Woman."

We were in a restaurant and I was shouting as if my integrity were at stake.

Howard turned in the screenplay to Twentieth Century-Fox. They read it almost overnight, but didn't feel it in their kishkas. They said, "Too mature. Where's the audience for this?" Howard took the screenplay to every other studio. It was universally rejected. But then some well-known actors read it and seemed to desire parts. The screenplay had an unusually large number of words, pages dark with type. It even opened with a talking head as the lead character tells a story. The actors might have liked the challenge of words, having to act, make an audience listen, survive the lingering scrutiny of the camera.

Using the actors' names, Howard could raise money independently, but months passed, the option on the novel lapsed, and it wasn't renewed. Everything seemed over; the work was lost. Howard became involved with another movie, but he phoned regularly. It wasn't over for him. He said money was coming in, a little here, a little there. This thing would not be allowed to die. I was skeptical and kept asking, "When is it going to happen?" He couldn't say, but he was positive it was going to happen.

From skepticism I fell into black doubt. There had been too many rejections. The screenplay was shopworn, passed around too much, soiled, cheapened. Not merely rejected; many disliked it. It wasn't a novel or a poem; the opinions of other people mattered. Worst of all, when I reread the screenplay, I didn't know what I felt about it. When one doesn't know writing is okay, it isn't okay, but there had been too much talk and praise and encouragement. There had also been tremendous work. More than anything work is destructive of judgment.

I once visited a monastery built by monks in the wilderness. They'd carved every stone by hand. It took them years to complete and they were very content with it, but their work was so brutally ugly that it seemed to comment on their faith. I wandered in halls and courtyard looking for a redeeming touch. There was no vision, no sensibility. In works of true self-abnegating faith, is there a necessary ugliness?

When Howard had laughed at lines, I laughed and felt great. To think I'd written *that*. Now, in the middle of the night, I'd wake up frightened, go to my desk, reread the screenplay and not know.

It was like waking up blind. I phoned my agent. "Is it good? Tell me the truth."

"It's good," he said. "It's a very valuable property."

Some friends read it and said it isn't good, others said it is. One friend, a film critic and scholar, said, "Look, the best screenplay in the world can be made into a lousy movie." Was the reverse also true? Harassing people with questions about essential value was futile. There was no truth.

Late winter, 1985, I went to the opening of two short plays by David Mamet, *Prairie du Chien* and *The Shawl*. They were about relations between imagination and reality, and the powers and terrors of estrangement in artists. The subject has been treated by Shakespeare, Byron, Blake, Kafka, and Wallace Stevens, among others. Mamet's plays seemed to me moving and very good. The next day, when critics attacked the plays, I thought only desire and luck prevailed in this world; maybe there had never been anything else. I felt a strange hope for my screenplay. If it wasn't good, could it be bad enough to succeed?

Other movie people approached me about the novel. Just the novel. One was brutally plain: "If they make that screenplay, with your name in the credits, you'll never work again." But if he made the novel a movie, I'd have artistic success. More money, too. I was immensely tempted, but never in my life have I succumbed to my own best interests. One evening in a bar, I pulled a five-by-eight file card from my briefcase, scribbled an option renewal agreement on it, signed my name, handed it to Howard. No lawyers, no agents, and drunk, I put an end to agonized indeterminacy. Like getting married not to deal with the excruciating prospect of backing out. Afterward you feel much better about yourself. G. Wilson Knight, the great Shakespearean critic, says Macbeth murders Duncan because he's afraid he might not. Hamlet acts similarly. I've rarely acted otherwise.

Money for a low-budget production was suddenly in the bank. A shooting schedule was drawn up and a date for rehearsals set. I was told to cancel whatever I was doing, make no further plans, be in Hollywood on that date. Since it was a low-budget production, no more fine hotels for me. I'd sleep in motels near the lot.

The lot, Hollywood Center, was crowded and hectic, movies in production all about. Gorgeous women strolled by like normal people. It came home to me that making movies was a way of life, and I was eager to begin, but a few days later I was kicked out.

I made the actors uneasy, inhibited their creative impulses. "We want to be alone with our director." I sat in the production office with nothing to do. Finally someone said, "Why don't you go back to Berkeley? You can read poems to pretty coeds. You don't really have to be here. Your script is so good they can't ruin it. Return when filming begins."

It's best if the writer isn't present, but I'd been told to be there, make no other plans, etc. Now I felt exiled. To explain this to friends in Berkeley was hard. One said, "Are your feelings hurt?"

"I don't feel great."

"But are your feelings hurt?"

Exiled from myself, too, I was unable to say my feelings were hurt. I languished for weeks in crepuscular gloom.

The director, Peter Medak, sometimes phoned. "Today the air-conditioning system broke down. It's the hottest summer in L.A. history. But everything is going well. You needn't be worried about your lines. The actors are saying only what you wrote, at least eighty percent."

Just before filming began, he said, "You're welcome, darling, but please don't come. I'll let you know how things are going. There's nothing to worry about. You're in reasonably good hands." Others phoned, too. I heard about disagreements over camera work, screaming fights on the set, blood on the walls, broken glass, teeth knocked out.

"What about the fighting, Peter?"

"It means people care. It's a good sign. What a courageous script. Such truth. Get your tux ready for the Academy Awards."

When the filming ended, I was reinvited to L.A.

On a hot dead Hollywood afternoon, in the summer of 1985, six years after I'd submitted a story called "The Men's Club" to *Cosmopolitan*, I sat in a cool, comfortable screening room and watched the rough-cut version of the movie.

"That it should come to this," says Hamlet. What force and point there is in "should." Today, we don't much use the word like that. A realm of human experience slips away from our language. I stood outside in the twilight waiting for Howard. When he came up, I said, "Can you reshoot some scenes?"

"There's no money in the budget to reshoot anything."

He was irritated. My question was more judgment than question. "Well," he said, "what should we do, kill ourselves?"

We were in it together, but I could feel only for myself. Disgrace, like internal bleeding, seeped into my bones and organs. As we walked toward the production office, he said, "Don't tell anyone what you think about the movie."

Oh, the rough cut wasn't all that bad. There were excellent performances. But that night, alone in my motel room, I watched the whole movie again, as I would for months thereafter when I was alone. Of one thing in the world I was sure. There was truth.

I saw it in the cracked tile about the bathtub, mildew in the walls, paint that bulged and split, a faucet that dribbled like an idiot, disease-yellow stains in the bedspread, and the pressure of squalid light when I turned on the lamp beside the bed. All mine; of my soul. The wicked, says Plato, shall suffer in this life just being what they are. I'd been very wicked, and now it astonished me, the tears, the ferociousness of my shame.

The motel wasn't far from Fairfax Avenue. Old men in dapper gabardines walked about long after midnight. They couldn't sleep, had nothing to do but wait for morning, then sip hot water and lemon, read the *Los Angeles Times*, nibble a prune Danish. Some wore hats, a touch of style, formal and jaunty, from the optimistic forties. Dear God, as You know, I wanted to be old, too. Need so little. I wouldn't resent the young their burning, but only pity its disgustingness, the lust there is in breathing, the predatory brightness of their movie eyes. Give me cataracts. Put them on the eyes of my soul, where the movie kept playing.

I'd described one character as having a slight speech defect. The actor came on with a sickeningly violent stutter. His stuttering hurt, like a gratuitous personal insult, so much that it felt deserved.

They said a rough cut is always terrible. Movies are made in the editing room. We had miles and miles of film. A good movie had only to be discovered in those miles of film. I was invited to help with the editing. I flew back and forth between Berkeley and L.A., grateful to be allowed to help. About ten scenes were cut, which had dire effects on structure, but the movie gained lunging energy and speed. It improved. Then disagreements flared once more. Somebody was fired. Somebody quit.

As the movie changed, gradually becoming the thing for which no more could be done, I went down to L.A. less frequently, then finally stopped. I missed hanging out at the Formosa bar after work, and eating dinner at the Chianti, the Rose, and Joe Allen's. I missed the glaring nighttime anxiety of Sunset Boulevard and the languid sweep of Santa Monica Boulevard from Hollywood through the imperial quietude of Beverly Hills and on to the grandeur of the Pacific, and also the deep mystery of San Vicente, how it bends and thrusts from lovely neighborhoods to eerie desolation. A dozen times I got lost and had to ask for help.

"You're looking for Melrose? It's right around here. It used to be somewhere else, but listen, baby, I moved a couple of years ago."

Avenues and streets were a gigantic nervous system, flashed with excitements, congealed with neurotic atmospheres or dull, dry, oppressive peacefulness. I missed L.A. like an old strange friend.

With a few exceptions, reviews were bludgeoningly bad.

Ten days after the movie opened, Howard phoned.

"The movie is dead."

"That's depressing."

"Nobody can feel worse than I do."

I thought I could. When he said good-bye, I would feel lonely, abandoned to reviewers, like a rape victim who not only suffers the opinions of cops but also feels guilty. I tried to keep talking, not let him hang up. It was no use. He managed a closing line.

"Well, we had some fun, didn't we?"

Published as "Kishkas" in *Partisan Review* and later adapted as "Movie Eyes" in *To Feel These Things* (Mercury House, 1993).

writing about myself

NOTHING SHOULD BE EASIER than talking about ways in which I write about myself, but I find it isn't at all easy. Indeed, in writing about myself I encounter a problem that engages me even as I write this sentence. The problem is how not to write merely about myself. I think the problem is endemic among writers whether or not they are aware of it. The basic elements of writing—diction, grammar, tone, imagery, the patterns of sound made by your sentences—say a good deal about you, so that it is possible for you to be writing about yourself before you even know you are writing about yourself. Regardless of your subject, the basic elements, as well as countless and immeasurable qualities of mind, are at play in your writing and will make your presence felt to a reader as palpably as your handwriting. You virtually write your name, as it were, before you literally sign your name, every time you write.

Spinoza wrote his *Ethics* in Latin, a language nobody spoke anymore, using a severely logical method of argument. The last thing he wanted was to make his presence felt, or to write about himself. The way he wrote his *Ethics* was rather like the way he lived, determined to remain obscure, uncompromised by a recognizable identity in the public world. The impersonal purity of his *Ethics*, then, couldn't have been more self-expressive. The book wasn't published in his lifetime, partly because it would have been recognized as his book. In his obscurity, he was too well known.

Shakespeare isn't discoverable in a personal way in anything he wrote, and yet it is generally agreed that we know what Shakespeare wrote, or what only he is likely to have written. His sonnets, which are among the most personal poems ever written, are remarkably artificial in their quatrains, couplets, puns, and paradoxes, devices that are manifestly impersonal. It is curiously relevant that, in Shakespeare's various signatures, he never spelled his name the same way twice, rather as if he thought his personal identity had very little to do with a particular way of spelling his name. A particular way would simply be individual.

Montaigne said of his essays, "I have no more made this book than this book has made me." I think he means his writing revealed him to himself, and the revelations weren't always consciously intended. Again and again in his essays he seems to discover himself inadvertently, which is to say only that your radically personal identity, with or without your consent, is made evident in your writing. Like a fingerprint. Or, what is even more personally telling, a face print: according to experts, there are eighty places in the human face that can be used to identify a person. These whorls and aspects are unique, if not exactly personal in the same way as your sentence structure.

One rainy night many years ago, I went with a friend to a jazz club called Basin Street in Greenwich Village to hear a Miles Davis quartet. There was a small, sophisticated crowd. It applauded in the right places. At a certain point Miles Davis began turning his back to the crowd whenever he played a solo. I don't know what he thought he was doing, but the effect was to absent himself from the tune, as though he were saying, "Don't look at me. I'm not here. Listen to it." He gave us a lesson in music appreciation, or the appreciation of any art. With Davis's back turned, the music became more personal.

A professor of mathematics at Berkeley told me that, while reading a newspaper article about the Unabomber, he suddenly realized the man had been his student. The professor then went to his files, pulled out the Unabomber's math papers and reviewed them. He said, "B/B+." Mathematics couldn't be further from the kinds of self-presentation and self-revelation to which all of us are constantly susceptible, but even in the absolutely neutral language of equations, the Unabomber had declared his identity. From the point of view of a mathematician, B/B+ was the man.

I think we name ourselves, more or less, whenever we write, and thus tend always to write about ourselves. When people ask if you write by hand or use a typewriter or a computer, they are interested to know how personal your writing is. But even now in the age of electronic writing when the revelations of handwriting have become rare, a ghostly electronic residue of persons remains faintly discernible in words and sentence structure. A more familiar example of what I'm getting at are phone calls. Imagine answering the phone and hearing a voice you haven't heard in years, a voice that says only your name or even only hello, and you say instantly, "Aunt Molly, it's been so long since you phoned." There's a joke that touches on this experience: The phone rings. Molly says, "Hello," and a man's voice says, "Molly, I know you and I know what you want. I'm coming over there and I'm going to throw you on the floor and do every dirty thing to you." Molly says, "You know all this from hello?"

In another kind of personal revelation, you see a picture that you've never seen before and you say, "Hokusai," or "Guercino," or "Cranach." With the names you announce that you have recognized a unique presence. The sheer existence of a human being, let alone personal presence in an artist's style, tends to be an announcement, virtually a name. This is no less true of my uncelebrated aunt Molly than the great and famous Hokusai. Adam was required to name the animals, but how could he have done that unless their names were already implicit in their individual being? Obviously, this beast is Lion, and this can only be Pig. In regard to animals the case is more individual than personal, as far as we know. If an animal could spell its name, it would be spelled the same way every time. Existence moves in the direction of names.

Diction, grammar, imagery, the sound of a person's voice on the phone, the way an animal looks—if a thing has any sort of sensational existence, a name is being announced, and this is true even if it goes unrecognized. It is God who says, "I am that I am," and remains nameless, accessible only through the *via negativa*. As Spinoza puts it, substance is conceived only in and through itself; that is, only in terms of itself. As for us folks, or any other finite individual entity, we are among the modes of substance and, ultimately, "rolled round in earth's diurnal course with rocks and stones and trees." This mournful line is from Wordsworth's profoundly personal poem about a woman who is never named. What makes the poem so haunting is that, regardless of the woman who is its subject, it is almost entirely, and desperately, about Wordsworth. Inevitably, we are names or nothing. To say Henry IV or John

Smith III is to say a name that precedes the being it names. The fourth Henry, the third John Smith.

I once wrote a story in which I quoted a freshman theme that had been submitted to my class. The student wrote: "Karl Marx, for that was his name . . ." It's as if Marx's father had said to his wife, "I've decided to name our boy Karl," and his wife said, "No, no, anything but Karl," and the father said, "I'm afraid I have no choice, for that is his name."

For reasons I understand very imperfectly, though I suppose they are obvious to anyone else by this point, it has always been more difficult for me to write about myself than any other subject. What I know for sure is that writing about myself always entails writing about other people, and there is a chance someone will be embarrassed or hurt even if my intentions are innocent. According to the Torah, this is an extremely serious sin. After death everyone goes to Gehenna, but only those who have not "embarrassed their neighbor" ever come back.

One of my brightest and most likeable students was named Canterbury. He wanted me to direct his dissertation. I told him that he ought to ask one of my colleagues who is well known as a scholar or critic, and has connections and will help him get a job. No. Canterbury wanted me to be the director. Finally, I agreed. Canterbury wrote a brilliant prospectus, and then became amazingly casual about the prospect of writing any more. Eventually, he left for West Virginia, his home state, where he made a name for himself in politics. Like Miles Davis, he'd turned his back on the audience that was me. Canterbury had to escape individual distinction, to achieve something personal. Before he left for West Virginia, I asked him to find a certain kind of old handmade tool, an adze, and bring it to me when he visited California. About six months later he presented me with the tool used in *As I Lay Dying* to make a coffin. I was very touched. Nothing remained of our professor-student relationship. We had become purely friends.

When I was writing my novel *The Men's Club*, it occurred to me that Canterbury was the right name for one of the characters. The character looked nothing like the real Canterbury, and his personality couldn't be more different, but my friend, the real Canterbury, was shocked. How could I have done this to him? "So that's what you think about me," he said. He went on and on reminding me of what I had done to him. I couldn't tell if he was serious.

Usually, when writing about myself, I will disguise the people I talk about and never use their real names. Occasionally, when I want to say something innocuous or affectionate, I'll ask permission to use the real name. One of my writer friends, also a former student, found it mysteriously impossible not to use real names when writing about herself, though it could make no difference to the quality or the sale of her book. She simply couldn't bring herself to change the names. As a result, people were hurt and family relations were irreparably damaged. There is something horrific about seeing your name in print. For some of us, it's almost as disturbing as a photograph. Even when writing only about myself, I'm reluctant to use my name in a sentence and I do it only when I have no choice. It gives me the creeps to write "Leonard" or "Lenny," except in letters.

I think I know why my student couldn't help using real names despite the consequences for her family relations. In my experience when writing about myself, the moment I begin making up names for the real people in my life, there seems to be a loss of seriousness, and then I can't get rid of the feeling and everything begins to seem like a lie, even if everything—except for a few names—is true. The impulse toward truth is built into our existence just as the shape of our eyes is built into our genes, and the truth, like murder, wants out. My friend should have changed the names of the real people in her book, but she couldn't do it. She was possessed by a sort of demonic righteousness. "I'm writing the truth and nothing but. These are the true names." People often say, when accused of slanderous gossip, "But it's the truth," as if that were a justification.

Another reason I have trouble writing about myself, aside from what it entails in regard to other people, has to do with the essential nature of writing. As Freud says, "Writing is the record of an absent person," which is a condensation of what Socrates said about not writing. He said, if you have something to say, you ought to be present to answer questions from your audience, because truth lies only in the practice of the dialectic and is extremely difficult to seize. When it happens, it is like a sudden flame. In Plato's seventh letter, he goes on about the frivolousness that is inevitable to writing, and says that any man who tries to write the truth, as it is known to himself, must be insane. There is no better definition of insanity.

Freud's way of restating Socrates' point, "the record of an absent person," is very suggestive. If you are absent when you write, it follows that you must be absent to the second power when you write about yourself. I'm trying to reconcile the idea of presence when writing about oneself with the Socratic-Freudian idea of absence at the heart of writing, itself. First a joke that touches on the dreadful complexity of simultaneous presence and absence:

The king and his court are out hunting elk in the royal forest. A poacher sees them coming and becomes terrified. He leaps from behind a bush and cries, "I am not an elk." Immediately, the king shoots him. One of the courtiers says, "But, Your Majesty, he said, 'I am not an elk.' " The king slaps his forehead and says, "I thought he said, 'I am an elk.' "

When I write anything my presence and absence are in tension. It becomes extreme when writing about myself. What makes things worse for me is that, because of this tension, I feel very much out of fashion, since it is now common for writers to be more than usually present, even outrageously present, in their writing, whether or not they are writing about themselves. Some writers don't know how to be otherwise than fully present. There has never been such extraordinary directness and candor. The effect is comparable to pornography—not because of explicit sexual content, but rather because such directness and candor tends to be shockingly impersonal.

The way I write about myself or anything else is, I'm afraid, personal or it's nothing. This means I must always find some appropriate form. One example of being personal and finding an appropriate form can be seen in Hamlet's famous soliloquy in which he thinks about suicide. He says, "That it should come to this." As opposed to Hamlet, a contemporary in the same situation might say, "Incredible," or some version of "Incredible," which is a cry of me-feeling.

The difference between the contemporary speaker and Hamlet isn't simply in the loss of the subjunctive mood but rather the loss of a significant intervening form between speaker and audience. When Hamlet says, "That it should come to this," he is noticing the convergence of terrific forces outside himself. One force is justice. The other is necessity. A grammatical form, the subjunctive mood, makes it possible for the reader and Hamlet to convene in the understanding of his personal situation. This convening is the experience of the personal. In order for it to have happened, Hamlet absents himself in the sentence as definitively as Miles Davis turning his back to the audience.

When the contemporary says, "Incredible," we are forbidden to convene in any understanding and obliged merely to notice a figure of emotion, all of which emotion is locked within his cry, "Incredible." This kind of expression, where meaning and feeling are at once sensationally apparent and completely unavailable to you, resembles greed. I take this to be emblematic of much contemporary writing and also much else that is contemporary. It's probably somehow related to the culture of capitalism, in which we are incessantly assaulted by images of things that we can't have, mainly beautiful faces and bodies, but also a lot of other things—vast fortunes, celebrity, power, love—almost anything you suppose people want.

The haiku, a poem of three lines and seventeen syllables that is usually about nature, offers a form in which writer and reader personally convene. I can't write haikus, but, when writing about myself, I feel the impulse to write in that terse and essentializing way. This is the intended form of my book *Time Out of Mind*, a selection of journal entries made over thirty years. In these entries I say more about myself personally than in any other place. I also say less since the entries contain far more implication than explication. For example, I made an entry on December 12, 1993, in Hawaii, that reads:

Birdcalls wake me, a sound like names, like the trees repeating themselves in the dawn mist, each holding its place, awaiting recognition, like names.

The context for this entry is omitted. A reader could figure it out somewhat from things said in other entries, though many autobiographical details that might seem relevant to a biographer or a gossip aren't given. I don't say that I woke up beside my girlfriend, who was twenty-seven years younger than me and would soon leave me, which I knew, though I didn't know she would leave me for a businessman.

My girlfriend and I had gone to Hawaii, the Puna coast of the Big Island. We were staying in one room of a primitive but elegant shack in an artists' colony. The shack had no windows. You could sense the magnificent luxuriance and vitality outside, the trees, the weather, the light, the ocean. In the other room of the shack, there were three men. One of them coughed all night. He had AIDS and so did several other men at the colony. The wall between our rooms was a thin sheet of wood. Listening to him cough, and knowing my girlfriend would leave me, are elements of the journal entry, and a reader might get a sense of them from other entries, but they aren't emphasized. I don't say that her youth didn't make me feel young, but rather the opposite, and I don't say that the coughing all night was heartbreaking and that it intensified the heartbreak I'd begun to feel, knowing I was much closer to the end than my girlfriend and knowing she would soon leave me. I don't say that, in the beginning of our love affair, she said she would never leave me. I don't say that I didn't pity myself, but felt an overwhelming melancholy. I say only that the birdcalls and the trees were like names. I watched the trees emerging in the mist, and I listened to the birdcalls. I was struck by the repetition of things and by the pathos there is in the way individual being is always emerging and calling its name as if to distinguish itself amid the mindless proliferation and density of life in general.

I don't say much of this in the journal. When writing about myself, I find that I am interested in the expressive value of form and its relation to the personal more than I am interested in particular revelations of my individual life.

Delivered as a talk called "The Personal and the Individual" at a conference on autobiographical writing, sponsored by *Partisan Review*, in Boston, in fall 2000. Later published under the same name in *Partisan Review*, January 2001.

my yiddish

IN PARIS ONE MORNING in the seventies, walking along the rue Mahler, I saw a group of old men in an argument, shouting and gesticulating. I wanted to know what it was about, but my graduate-school French was good enough only to read great writers, not good enough for an impassioned argument or even conversation with the local grocer. But then, as I walked by the old men, I felt a shock and a surge of exhilaration. I did understand them. My God, I possessed the thing: spoken French! Just as suddenly, I crashed. The old men, I realized, were shouting in Yiddish.

Like a half-remembered dream, the incident lingered. It seemed intensely personal yet impersonal. Meaning had come alive in me. I hadn't translated what the old men said. I hadn't done anything. A light turned on. Where nothing had been, there was something.

Philosophers used to talk about "The Understanding" as if it were a distinct mental function. Today they talk about epistemology or cognitive science. As for "The Understanding," it's acknowledged in IQ tests, the value of which is subject to debate. It's also acknowledged in daily life in countless informal ways. You're on the same wavelength with others or you are not. The Paris incident, where I rediscovered The Understanding, made me wonder if Descartes' remark "I think, therefore I am" might be true in his case, but not mine. I prefer to say, "I am, therefore I think." And also, therefore, I speak.

Until I was five, I spoke only Yiddish. It did much to permanently qualify my thinking. Eventually I learned to speak English, then to imitate thinking as it transpires among English-speakers. To some extent, my intuitions and my expression of thoughts remain basically Yiddish. I can say only approximately how this is true. For example, this joke:

The rabbi says, "What's green, hangs on the wall, and whistles?"

The student says, "I don't know."

The rabbi says, "A herring."

The student says, "Maybe a herring could be green and hang on the wall, but it absolutely doesn't whistle."

The rabbi says, "So it doesn't whistle."

The joke is inherent in Yiddish, not any other language. It's funny and, like a story by Kafka, it isn't funny. I confess that I don't know every other language. Maybe there are such jokes in Russian or Chinese, but no other language has a history like Yiddish, which, for ten centuries, has survived the dispersion and murder of its speakers.

As the excellent scholar and critic Benjamin Harshav points out, in *The Meaning of Yiddish*, the language contains many words that don't mean anything: *nu, epes, tockeh, shoyn*. These are fleeting interjections, rather like sighs. They suggest, without meaning anything, "so," "really," "well," "already." Other Yiddish words and phrases, noticed by Harshav, are meaningful but defeat translation. Transparent and easy to understand, however, is the way Yiddish serves speech—between you and me—rather than the requirements of consecutive logical discourse; that is, between the being who goes by your name and who speaks to others objectively and impersonally. For example, five times five is twenty-five, and it doesn't whistle.

Yiddish is probably at work in my written English. This moment, writing in English, I wonder about the Yiddish undercurrent. If I listen, I can almost hear it: "This moment"—a stress followed by two neutral syllables—introduces a thought that hangs like a herring in the weary droop of "writing in English," and then comes the announcement, "I wonder about the Yiddish undercurrent." The sentence ends in a shrug. Maybe I hear the Yiddish undercurrent, maybe I don't. The sentence could have been written by anyone who knows English, but it probably would not have been written by a well-bred Gentile. It has too much drama, and might even be disturbing, like music in a restaurant or elevator. The sentence obliges you to abide in its staggered flow, as if what I meant were inextricable from my feelings and required a lyrical note. There is a kind of enforced intimacy with the reader. A Jewish kind, I suppose. In Sean O'Casey's lovelier prose you hear an Irish kind.

Wittgenstein says in his *Philosophical Investigations*, "Aren't there games we play in which we make up the rules as we go along, including this one." *Nu.* Any Yiddish speaker knows that. A good example of playing with the rules might be Montaigne's essays, the form that people say he invented. *Shoyn*, a big inventor. Jews have always spoken essays. The scandal of Montaigne's essays is that they have only an incidental relation to a consecutive logical argument but they are cogent nonetheless. Their shape is their sense. It is determined by motions of his mind and feelings, not by a pretension to rigorously logical procedure. Montaigne literally claims his essays are himself. Between you and him nothing intervenes. A Gentile friend used to say, in regard to writing she didn't like, "There's nobody home." You don't have to have Jewish ancestors, like those of Montaigne and Wittgenstein, to understand what she means.

I didn't speak English until I was five because my mother didn't speak English. My father had established himself in New York in the twenties, then gone back to Poland to find a wife. He returned with an attractive seventeen-year-old who wore her hair in a long black braid. Men would hit on her, so my father wouldn't let her go take English classes. She learned English by doing my elementary-school homework with me. As for me, before and after the age of five, I was susceptible to lung diseases and spent a lot of time in a feverish bed in a small apartment on the Lower East Side of Manhattan, where nobody spoke anything but Yiddish. Years passed before I could ride a bike or catch a ball. In a playground fight, a girl could have wiped me out. I was badly coordinated and had no strength or speed, only a Yiddish mouth.

For a long time, Yiddish was my whole world. In this world family didn't gather before dinner for cocktails and conversation. There were no cocktails, but conversation was daylong and it included criticism, teasing, opinionating, gossiping, joking. It could also be very gloomy. To gather before dinner for conversation would have seemed unnatural. I experienced the pleasure of such conversation for the first time at the University of Michigan around 1956. It was my habit to join a friend at his apartment after classes. He made old-fashioneds and put music on the phonograph, usually chamber music. By the time we left for dinner, I felt uplifted by conversation and splendid music. Mainly, I was drunk, also a new experience. Among my Jews, conversation had no ritual character, no aesthetic qualities. I never learned to cultivate the sort of detachment that allows for the always potentially offensive personal note. Where I came from everything was personal.

From family conversation I gathered that, outside of my Yiddish child-world, there were savages who didn't have much to say but could fix the plumbing. They were fond of animals, liked to go swimming, loved to drink and fight. All their problems were solved when they *hut geharget yiddin*. Killed Jews. Only the last has been impossible for me to dismiss. Like many other people, I have fixed my own plumbing, owned a dog and a cat, gotten drunk, etc., but everything in my life, beginning with English, has been an uncertain movement away from my *hut geharget* Yiddish childhood. When a BBC poet said he wanted to shoot Jews on the West Bank, I thought, "*Epes*. What else is new?" His righteousness, his freedom to say it, suggests that he believes he is merely speaking English and anti-Semitism is a kind of syntax, or what Wittgenstein calls "a form of life." But in fact there is something new, or anyhow more evident lately. The *geharget yiddin* disposition now operates at a remove. You see it in people who become hysterical when their ancient right to hate Jews is brought into question. To give an example would open a boxcar of worms.

It's possible to talk about French without schlepping the historical, cultural, or national character of a people into consideration. You cannot talk that way about Yiddish unless you adopt a narrow scholarly focus, or restrict yourself to minutiae of usage. The language flourished in a number of countries. Theoretically, it has no territorial boundary. The meaning of Yiddish, in one respect, is No

Boundaries. In another respect, for a people without a land, the invisible boundaries couldn't be more clear. There is mutual contempt between what are called "universalist Jews" and Jewish Jews. It's an old situation. During the centuries of the Spanish Inquisition, Jews turned on Jews. In Shakespeare's *The Merchant of Venice*— assuming the merchant Antonio is a gay converso, or new Christian, and Shylock is an Old Testament moralistic Jewish Jew— the pound of flesh, a grotesquely exaggerated circumcision, is to remind Antonio (who says, "I know not why I am so sad") of his origins.

The first time I went to a baseball game, the great slugger Hank Greenberg, during warm-up, casually tossed a ball into the stands, a gift to the crowd of preadolescent kids among whom I sat. My hand, thrusting up in a blossom of hands, closed on that baseball. I carried it home, the only palpable treasure I'd ever owned. I never had toys. On Christmas nights I sometimes dreamed of waking and finding toys in the living room. *Tokeh?* Yes, really. If there is a support group for Christmas depressives, I will be your leader. The baseball made me feel like a real American. It happened to me long before I had a romance with the mythical blond who grants citizenship to Jews. By then I was already fifteen. I had tasted *traif* and long ago stopped speaking Yiddish except when I worked as a waiter in Catskill hotels. What Yiddish remained was enough for jokes, complaints, and insults. As guests entered the dining room, a waiter might say, "Here come the *vildeh chayes*," or wild animals. One evening in the Catskills I went to hear a political talk given in Yiddish. I understood little except that Yiddish could be a language of analysis, spoken by intellectuals. I felt alienated and rather ashamed of myself for not being like them.

Family members could speak Polish as well as Yiddish, and

some Hebrew and Russian. My father worked for a short while in Paris and could manage French. My mother had gone to high school in Poland and was fluent in Polish, but refused to speak the language even when I asked her to. Her memory of pogroms made it unspeakable. In Yiddish and English I heard about her father, my grandfather, a tailor who made uniforms for Polish army officers. Once, after he'd worked all night to finish a uniform, the officer wouldn't pay. My grandfather, waving a pair of scissors, threatened to cut the uniform to pieces. The officer paid. The Germans later murdered my grandfather, his wife, and one daughter. Polish officers imprisoned in Katyn Forest and elsewhere were massacred by Stalin. This paragraph, beginning with the first sentence and concluding with a moral, is in the form of a *geshichte*, or Yiddish story, except that it's in English and merely true.

At the center of my Yiddish, lest I have yet failed to make myself clear, remains *hut geharget yiddin*, from which, like the disgorged contents of a black hole in the universe, come the jokes, the thinking, the meanings, and the meaninglessness. In 1979, American writers were sent to Europe by the State Department. I went to Poland and gave talks in Warsaw, Poznań, and Cracow. I was surprised by how much seemed familiar, and exceedingly surprised by the intelligence and decency of the Poles, a few of whom became friends and visited me later in America. One of the Poles whom I didn't see again was a woman in Cracow with beautiful blue eyes and other features very like my mother's. I was certain that she was a Jew, though she wore a cross. I didn't ask her questions. I didn't want to know her story. I could barely look at her. I detest the word "shiksa," which I've heard used more often by friendly anti-Semites than Jews, but in my personal depths it applies to her.

As suggested earlier, in Yiddish there is respect for meaninglessness. If the woman in Cracow was passing as a Catholic, was she therefore a specter of meaninglessness who haunted me, the child of Polish Jews, passing as an American writer? A familiar saying comes to mind: "If you forget you are a Jew, a Gentile will remind you," but, in the way of forgetting, things have gone much further. Lately, it might take a Jew to remind a Jew that he or she is a Jew. Then there is a risk of ruining the friendship. For an extreme example, I have had depressing arguments with Jewish Stalinists who, despite evidence from numerous and unimpeachable sources that Stalin murdered Jews because they were Jews, remain Stalinists. It's as if they would rather die than let personal identity spoil their illusions. Thus, the Jewish face of insanity says to me, "Stalin was a good guy. He just got a bad rap." A demonic parallel to this mentality is in the way Nazis used material resources, critical to their military effort, to murder Jews even as the Russian army was at the gates. They would rather die, etc. In the second century, Tertullian, a Father of the Christian church, insisted that absurdity is critical to belief. His political sophistication seems to me breathtaking, and also frightening in its implications. As believers multiply everywhere, it becomes harder to believe—rationally—in almost anything.

Paradox as a cognitive mode is everywhere in Yiddish. It's probably in the genes and may explain the Jewish love of jokes. The flight from sense to brilliance effects an instant connection with listeners. Hobbes calls laughter "sudden glory," which is a superb phrase, but I've seen the Jewish comics, Lenny Bruce and Myron Cohen, reduce a nightclub audience to convulsive and inglorious agonies of laughter. When I worked in the Catskill hotels, I noticed that it was often the *tumler*, or the hotel comic and hell-raiser, to whom women abandoned themselves. Jerry Lewis, formerly a *tum-*

ler, said in a televised interview that at the height of his fame, he "had four broads a day." As opposed to Jerry Lewis, Hannah Arendt preferred disconnection. She used the snobbish-aesthetic word "banal" to describe the murderer of millions of Jews, and later said in a letter, despite the abuse she received for having used that word, she remained "lighthearted." Not every Jew is in the same league as Jerry Lewis, but still, with Arendt one could die laughing.

Family was uncles and aunts who escaped from Poland and immigrated to the United States. They stayed with us until they found their own apartments. I'd wake in the morning and see small Jews sleeping on the living-room floor. My aunt Molly, long after she had a place of her own, often stayed overnight and slept on the floor. She was very lonely. Her husband was dead, her children had families of their own. A couch with a sheet, blanket, and pillow was available, but she refused such comforts. She wanted to be less than no trouble. She wore two or three dresses at once, almost her entire wardrobe. She slept on the floor in her winter coat and dresses. To see Molly first thing in the morning, curled against a wall, didn't make us feel good. She was the same height as my mother, around five feet, and had a beautiful, intelligent, melancholy face. I never saw her laugh, though she might chuckle softly, and she smiled when she teased me. She used to *krotz* (scratch) my back as I went to sleep, and she liked to speak to me in rhymes. First they were entirely Yiddish. Then English entered the rhymes:

Label, gay fressen.
A fish shtayt on de tish.

Lenny, go eat.
A fish is on the table.

Shtayt doesn't exactly mean "is." "Stands on the table," or "stays on the table," or "exists on the table" would be somewhat imprecise, though I think "A fish exists on the table" is wonderful. I once brought a girlfriend home, and Aunt Molly said, very politely, "You are looking very fit." Her "fit" sounded like "fet," which suggested "fat." My girlfriend squealed in protest. It took several minutes to calm her down. The pronunciation of "fet" for "fit" is typical of Yiddishified English, which is almost a third language. I speak it like a native when telling jokes. The audience for such jokes has diminished over the years because most Jews now are politically liberal and have college degrees and consider such jokes undignified or racist. A joke that touches on this development tells of Jewish parents who worry about a son who studies English literature at Harvard. They go to see Kittredge, the great Shakespeare scholar, and ask if he thinks their son's Yiddish accent is a disadvantage. Kittredge booms, "Vot ekcent?"

As a child I knew only one Jew who was concerned to make a *bella figura*. He was a highly respected doctor, very handsome, always dressed in a fine suit, and, despite his appearance, fluent in Yiddish. His office was in the neighborhood. He came every morning to my father's barber shop for a shave. A comparable miracle was the chicken-flicker down the block, a boisterous man who yelled at customers in vulgar, funny Yiddish. This man's son was a star at MIT. In regard to such miracles, an expression I often heard was "He is up from pushcarts." It means he went from the Yiddish immigrant poverty to money or, say, a classy professorship. The day of such expressions is past. In the sixties there were Jewish kids who, as opposed to the spirit of Irving Howe's *The World of Our Fathers*, yelled "Kill the parents." The suicidal implication is consistent with the paradoxical Yiddish they no longer spoke.

If I dressed nicely to go out, my mother would ask why I was *fapitzed*, which suggests "tarted up." Yiddish is critical of pretensions to being better than a Jew, and also critical of everything else. A man wants to have sex or wants to pee—what a scream. A woman appears naked before her husband and says, "I haven't got a thing to wear." He says, "Take a shave. You look like a bum." Henry Adams speaks of "derisive Jew laughter." It is easy to find derision produced by Jews, but Adams's words, aside from their stupid viciousness, betray the self-hate and fear that inspires anti-Semitism among the educated, not excluding Jews. Ezra Pound called his own anti-Semitic ravings "stupid." The relation of stupidity and evil has long been noted.

Jewish laughter has a liberal purview, and its numerous forms—some very silly—seem to me built into Yiddish. Sometime around puberty, I decided to use shampoo rather than hand soap to wash my hair. I bought a bottle of Breck. My father noticed and said in Yiddish, "Nothing but the best." I still carry his lesson in my heart, though I never resumed using hand soap instead of shampoo. What has shampoo to do with Yiddish? In my case, plenty, since it raises the question, albeit faintly, "Who do you think you are?"

What I have retained of Yiddish, I'm sorry to say, isn't much above the level of my aunt Molly's poems. But what good to me is Yiddish? Recently, in Rome during the High Holidays, a cordon was established around the synagogue in the ghetto, guarded by the police and local Jews. As I tried to pass I was stopped by a Jew. Couldn't he tell? I said, *"Ich bin a yid. Los mir gayen arein."* He said, "Let me see your passport." *La mia madra lingua* wasn't his. This happened to me before with Moroccan Jews in France. I've wondered about Spinoza. His Latin teacher was German, and the first Yiddish newspaper was published in Amsterdam around the time of his death. Is it possible that he didn't know Yiddish?

I'm sure of very little about what I know except that the Yiddish I can't speak is more natural to my being than English. Partly for that reason I've studied poets writing in English. There is a line in T. S. Eliot where he says words slip, slide, crack, or something. "Come off it, Tom," I think. "With words you never had no problem." Who would suspect from his hateful remark about a Jew in furs that Eliot's family, like my mother's ancestors in Vienna, was up from the fur business? Eliot liked Groucho Marx, a Jew, but did Eliot wonder when writing *Four Quartets*, with its striking allusions to Saint John of the Cross, that the small, dark, brilliant, mystical monk might have been a Jew?

"Let there be light" are the first spoken words in the Old Testament. This light is understanding, not merely seeing. The Yiddish saying "To kill a person is to kill a world" means the person is no longer the embodiment, or a mode of the glorious nothing that is the light, or illuminated world. This idea, I believe, is elaborated in Spinoza's *Ethics*. Existence—or being—entails ethics. Maybe the idea is also in Wittgenstein, who opens the *Tractatus* this way: "The world is everything that is the case." So what is the case? If it's the case that facts are bound up with values, it seems Yiddish or Spinozist. Possibly for this reason Jewish writers in English don't write about murder as well as Christians. Even Primo Levi, whose great subject is murder, doesn't offer the lacerating specificity one might expect.

In regard to my own writing, its subterranean Yiddish may keep me from being good at killing characters in my stories. The closest I've come is my story "Trotsky's Garden," where I adopt a sort of Yiddish intonation to talk about the murders that haunted his life. I'd read a psychological study that claimed Trotsky was responsible for murders only to please Lenin, his father figure. If so, his behavior was even worse than I thought. I wrote my story out of disappointment. I had wanted to admire Trotsky for his brilliant mind, courage, and extraordinary literary gifts. His description in his diaries of mowing wheat, for example, almost compares with Tolstoy's description in *Anna Karenina* and is difficult to reconcile with a life steeped in gore.

Yiddish can be brutal, as for example: *Gay koken aff yam*, which means "Go shit in the ocean," but in regard to murder, what Jewish writer compares with Shakespeare, Webster, Mark Twain, Flannery O'Connor, Cormac McCarthy, or Elmore Leonard? The Old Testament story of Abraham and Isaac, which is of profound importance to three faiths, stops short of murder, but it is relevant to children murdered in contemporary religious terrorism.

A story by Bernard Malamud begins with the death of a father whose name is Ganz. In Yiddish *ganz* means "all" or "the whole thing" or "everything." Metaphorically, with the death of Ganz, the whole world dies. Everything is killed. Malamud couldn't have named the father Ganz if he had written the story in Yiddish. It would be too funny and undermine all seriousness. The death of a father, or a world-killed-in-a-person, is the reason for Hamlet's excessive grief, a condition feared among Jews for a reason given in the play: "All the uses of this world seem to me weary, stale, flat, and unprofitable." Because Hamlet Senior is dead, Hamlet Junior is as good as dead. Early in the play he jokes about walking into his grave, and the fifth act opens, for no reason, with Hamlet in a graveyard, and then he actually jumps into a grave. On the subject of grief, in "Mourning and Melancholia," Freud follows Shakespeare. Like Hamlet, who demands that his mother look at the picture of his father, Freud makes a great deal of the residual, or cathectic, force of an image. Again, regarding my Yiddish, when I once wrote about my father's death, I restricted my grief to a few images and a simple lamentation: "He gave. I took." My short sentences are self-critical, and have no relation to writers known for short sentences. They are only Yiddish terseness seizing an English equivalent.

Shakespeare's short sentences—"Let it come down," "Ripeness is all," "Can Fulvia die?"—seem to me amazing. I couldn't write one of those. This confession brings a joke instantly to mind. The synagogue's janitor is beating his breast and saying, "Oh, Lord, I am nothing." He is overheard by the rabbi, who says, "Look who is nothing." Both men are ridiculed. A Jewish writer has to be careful. Between schmaltz and irony, there is just an itty-bitty step.

My mother sometimes switches in mid-sentence, when talking to me, from English to Yiddish. If meaning can leave English and reappear in Yiddish, does it have an absolutely necessary relation to either language? Linguists say, "No. Anything you can say in German you can say in Swahili, which is increasingly Arabic." But no poet would accept the idea of linguistic equivalence, and a religious fanatic might want to kill you for proposing it. Ultimately, I believe, meaning has less to do with language than with music, a sensuous flow that becomes language only by default, so to speak, and by degrees. In great fiction and poetry, meaning is always close to music. Writing about a story by Gogol, Nabokov says it goes la, la, do, la la la, etc. The story's meaning is radically musical. I've often had to rewrite a paragraph because the sound was wrong. When at last it seemed right, I discovered—incredibly—the sense was right. Sense follows sound. Otherwise, we couldn't speak so easily or quickly. If someone speaks slowly, and sense unnaturally precedes sound, the person can seem too deliberative, emotionally false, boring. I can tell stories all day, but to write one that sounds right entails labors of indefinable innerness until I hear the thing I must hear before it is heard by others. A standard of rightness probably exists for me in my residual subliminal Yiddish. Its effect is to inhibit as well as to liberate.

An expression popular not long ago, "I hear you," was intended to assure you of being understood personally, as if there were a difference in comprehension between hearing and really hearing. In regard to being *really* heard, there are things in Yiddish that can't be heard in English. *Hazar fisl kosher.* "A pig has clean feet." It is an expression of contempt for hypocrisy. The force is in Yiddish concision. A pig is not clean. With clean feet it is even less clean. Another example: I was talking to a friend about a famous, recently deceased writer. The friend said, "He's *ausgespielt.*" Beyond dead. He's played out. So forget it. Too much has been said about him.

Cultural intuitions, or forms or qualities of meaning, derive from the unique historical experience of peoples. The intuitions are not in dictionaries but carried by tones, gestures, nuances effected by word order, etc. When I understood the old men in Paris, I didn't do or intend anything. It wasn't a moment of romantic introspection. I didn't know what language I heard. I didn't understand that I understood. What comes to mind is the assertion that begins the book of John: "In the beginning was the word." A sound, a physical thing, the word is also mental. So this monism can be understood as the nature of everything. Like the music that is the meaning of stories, physical and mental are aspects of each other. Yiddish, with its elements of German, Hebrew, Aramaic, Latin, Spanish, Polish, Russian, Romanian, etc., is metaphorically everything. A people driven hither and yon, and obliged to assimilate so much, returned immensely more to the world. How they can become necessary to murder is the hideous paradox of evil.

When I was five years old, I started school in a huge gloomy Victorian building where nobody spoke Yiddish. It was across the street from Knickerbocker Village, the project in which I lived. To cross that street meant going from love to hell. I said nothing in the classroom and sat apart and alone, trying to avoid the teacher's evil eye. Eventually, she decided that I was a moron and wrote a letter to my parents saying I would be transferred to the "ungraded class," where I would be happier and could play Ping Pong all day. My mother couldn't read the letter so she showed it to our neighbor, a woman from Texas named Lynn Nations. A real American, she boasted of Indian blood, though she was blond and had the cheek-bones, figure, and fragility of a fashion model. She would ask us to look at the insides of her teeth and see how they were cupped. To Lynn this proved descent from original Americans. She was very fond of me, though we had no conversation, and I spent hours in her apartment looking at her art books and eating forbidden foods. I could speak to her husband, Arthur Kleinman, yet another furrier and a lefty union activist, who knew Yiddish.

Lynn believed I was brighter than a moron and went to the school principal, which my mother would never have dared to do, and demanded an intelligence test for me. Impressed by her Katharine Hepburn looks, the principal arranged for a school psy-chologist to test me. Afterward, I was advanced to a grade beyond my age with several other kids, among them a boy named Bonfiglio and a girl named Estervez. I remember their names because we were seated according to our IQ scores. Behind Bonfiglio and Estervez was me, a kid who couldn't even ask permission to go to the bathroom. In the higher grade I had to read and write and speak English. It happened virtually overnight, so I must have known more than I knew. When I asked my mother about this, she said, "Sure you knew English. You learned from trucks." She meant, while lying in my sickbed, I would look out the window at trucks passing in the street; studying the words written on their sides, I taught myself English. Unfortunately, high fevers burned away most of my brain, so I now find it impossible to learn a language from trucks. A child learns any language at incredible speed. Again, in a metaphorical sense, Yiddish is the language of children wandering for a thousand years in a nightmare, assimilating languages to no avail.

I remember the black shining print of my first textbook, and my fearful uncertainty as the meanings came with all their exotic Englishness and devoured what had previously inhered in my Yiddish. Something remained indigestible. What it is can be suggested, in a Yiddish style, by contrast with English. A line from a poem by Wallace Stevens, which I have discussed elsewhere, seems to me quintessentially goyish, or antithetical to Yiddish:

It is the word pejorative *that hurts.*

Stevens effects detachment from his subject, which is the poet's romantic heart, by playing on a French construction: "word *pejorative*," like *mot juste*, makes the adjective follow the noun. Detachment is further evidenced in the rhyme of "word" and "hurts." The delicate resonance gives the faint touch of hurtful impact without obliging the reader to suffer the experience. The line is ironically detached even from detachment. In Yiddish there is plenty of irony, but not so nicely mannered or sensitive to a reader's experience of words. Stevens's line would seem too self-regarding, and the luxurious subtlety of his sensibility would seem unintelligible if not ridiculous. He flaunts sublimities here, but it must be said that elsewhere he is as visceral and concrete as any Yiddish speaker.

I've lost too much of my Yiddish to know exactly how much remains. Something remains. If a little of its genius is at work in my sentences, it has nothing to do with me personally. Pleasures of complexity and the hilarity of idiocy, as well as an idea of what's good or isn't good, are in Yiddish. If it speaks in my sentences, it isn't I, let alone me, who speaks.

When asked what he would have liked to be if he hadn't been born an Englishman, Lord Palmerston said, "An Englishman." The answer reminds me of a joke. A Jew sees himself in a mirror after being draped in a suit by a high-class London tailor. The tailor asks what's wrong. The Jew says, crying, "Vee lost de empire." The joke assimilates the insane fury that influenced the nature of Yiddish and makes it apparent that identity for a Jew is not, as for Palmerston, a witty preference.

Published as "My Yiddish" in *The Threepenny Review*, Fall 2003, then republished as "My Yiddish" in *The Genius of Language*, edited and with an introduction by Wendy Lesser (Pantheon Books, 2004), and in *The Best American Essays of 2004*, edited and with an introduction by Louis Menand. Both of the latter two books were dedicated to Leonard Michaels. Except for a very few small changes, this version is consistent with the two published versions. "My Yiddish" is the last piece of writing that Lenny completed for publication before he became sick in April 2003.

Leonard Michaels (1933–2003) was the author of six collections of stories and essays as well as two novels, *Sylvia* and *The Men's Club*. His *Collected Stories* and novels are available as FSG Classics.